*B*LUEBERRYLAND

Blueberry rakers in the field.

After a successful day of raking blueberries.

BLUEBERRYLAND

Taming the Maine Wild Lowbush Blueberry

WALTER STAPLES

PETER E. RANDALL PUBLISHER
PORTSMOUTH, NEW HAMPSHIRE
2003

Blueberry drawing by Kathy Meader
Cover design: Grace Peirce

Library of Congress Control Number: 2003102977
ISBN: 1-931807-15-9

Peter E. Randall Publisher
Box 4726, Portsmouth, NH 03802
www.perpublisher.com

Distributed by
University Press of New England
            Hanover and London

BLUEBERRYLAND

My three year-old granddaughter, Alison, inadvertently provided the title for my book about blueberries.

The usual thick morning fog of Downeast August days, in which son Jim and I had started raking, had been absorbed by bright sunshine. It was nearing noon before Alison arrived with her mother, Rebekah, for her first berry picking adventure. When her mother started raking, I gave Alison a small rake, and though she did not, or could not, hold it in the usual manner required to scoop the berries off the low bushes, she developed a system that was apparently satisfactory to her. Standing in an area of heavily fruited bushes, clutching the rake in her left hand, she bent and picked the berries, one at a time, placing them carefully in the rake, until there were a dozen or more; then she straightened, and one at a time, proceeded to take the berries out and eat them.

She repeated the process, over and over, until noon, when we left the blueberry field and drove to camp. Alison's fingers, lips, and teeth were blue from the berries she had eaten, and she ate little before wandering about the room, while her mother, Jim, and I ate lunch.

After a while, she cuddled close to her mother and asked, '"When are we going back to *Blueberryland*?" She had connoted the word from the memory of having previously visited Storyland, an imaginative park for children, in the North Conway, New Hampshire, area.

CONTENTS

Acknowledgments

Except for New Hampshire winters, I would never have taken time from farming and fishing in the great out of doors to write of my experiences. Had I not met Alex Levin, I would never have written *Blueberryland*. Had it not been for the encouragement of relatives and members of a Snow Village Writers Group, I never would have finished the book. Natalie Peterson not only corrected my grammar, she took many of the pictures used in the book. David Yarborough, Blueberry Specialist at the University of Maine, provided much more information than I knew how to use.

Carola Day Nickerson of the Wesley Historical Society provided access to the town history including that in their publication, *The History of Wesley, Maine*. Personnel at the libraries of Machias and Ellsworth were exceptionally helpful in bringing pertinent information to my attention. Memories, and more, came from interviews with Bill and Nellie Hayward, Bill Guptill, and Herbert and Flo Hanscom.

My daughter, Diane, slaved over the computer while recording the multiple changes made in the manuscript, daughter Rebekah and her husband, Charlie, read and re-read as I constantly changed the wording and format in response to advice. Sons Jim and Russ and daughter Mary and other family members provided much transportation and support during the interviews and research. As at the beginning, Alex Levin returned to perform the frustrating task of editing what I was writing.

I deeply appreciate those mentioned, and many others who have helped.

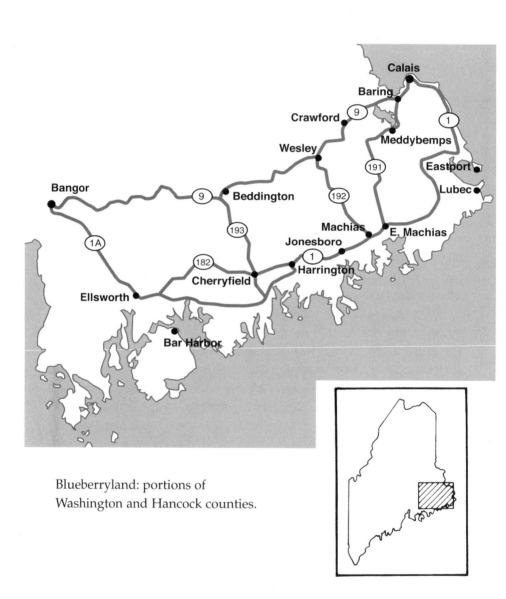

Blueberryland: portions of
Washington and Hancock counties.

Preface

The history of lowbush blueberry production in Maine is the story of 500 or more homesteads pioneered in the 1700s by settlers in a twenty mile-wide band inland and extending the entire length of its Atlantic coastline. Following the accepted practice of living off the land, not unlike the native Indians they replaced, survival depended on the trees from which they constructed and heated their homes to provide protection against the elements and wild animals. They cleared the land on which to grow grains and vegetables, and harvested the available wild meat, fruit, and berries.

Blueberries were one of the more widespread and plentiful berries, and the local Indian tribes had long before discovered the mother lode situated on the barrens. This was a near treeless area of eskers and meadows at the western edge of what has become Washington County along its boundary with Hancock County. Settlement was pressing inland from the seacoast villages during the 1700s, but it was not until the 1900s, when railroad transportation had penetrated the area and factories had learned to preserve the berries by canning, that blueberries became of economic importance and the growing area extended beyond the barrens.

It came about in Wesley at the time of, and because of, the end of the oxen and horsepower era of cutting the virgin timber. The huge fields necessary to grow the hay to feed the oxen and horses were no longer needed. It must have seemed a miracle to those remaining landowners with large families to see the lowbush blueberries spread over their fields, and to have agents from Cherryfield and Ellsworth canning factories come to offer cash for their berries. It provided cash income from the wild berries, not only for the men who had been cutting logs and driving the oxen and horses, but provided work for every family member, including children. They often made little money, but they never lost money, only saw less profit when the season was poor or the market price low.

Unlike when the girls left the farms to work in the cotton mills and machine factories, the blueberry growing families stayed together at home, each member participating in the work.

What I had intended and expected was for this book to be a compilation of unusual circumstances, anecdotes, and stories from my personal experience during a period of twenty years of managing a relatively small blueberry farm; inadvertently; it has become much more. It has become a description of an intimate association with the people and the land of the small town of Wesley in Washington County, Maine, a town not unlike every other blueberry growing town in the state. The industry developed over a period of fifty years from berries picked for family use to more than 100 million pounds produced annually and marketed internationally.

The development of herbicides, insecticides, and fertilizers, and the equipment to apply them; the sprayers, gas and oil burners, berry rakers and the tractors to power and move them; plus the costs of modern transportation, resulted in an exchange of labor income for the purchase or rental of such equipment; and the price paid the grower per pound of blueberries fluctuated from single digits to fifty cents or more. The grower also remained at the mercy of weather conditions, over which he had no control.

The instability of at least the smaller growers—of necessity part-time and under-financed, as well as ill-informed and ill-advised—questions their continued participation, but they own the land, as their fathers did, and there is little other use for the old fields. Somewhat like playing the lottery, next year will produce a bigger crop, and the price will be higher. Next year, next year.

Such contradictions and confusion may well be reflected in the way it is presented in *Blueberryland*.

PART I: DESTINY

The author in his field picking blueberries for personal use.

1

WITHOUT WARNING

I had left Crawford lake early. The fishing for small mouth bass had been particularly good. I had released five keepers, and kept a fourteen-inch one for dinner. The usual thick fog of an August morning in Washington County, Maine, had cleared, and a slight breeze warned of whitecaps soon to develop. Even more persuasive was the blue field of ripe berries on my land in Wesley, waiting to be picked. I had purchased the land about five years before, but arranged for the seller to maintain ownership of the blueberry crop for as long as he was basically able to manage it, as I had not retired from my full time position, which required a great deal of travel and responsibility. I retained permission for myself and family to harvest whatever amount of berries we wanted for personal use. I had arrived a few days early at the camp my sons and friends had helped me build on Nineteen Road. I had arrived early because mostly, I wanted to be the first to bend down on my knees and reach into that blue mass of berries—not to eat them—but to loosen them with my fingers, and drop them one by one into the quart baskets. I never ate berries when picking them, a lesson learned from my father who had insisted that my pail, or whatever container I had used, must be filled before I ate a single one. Now that day in August had come again, as it had for the past five years, and I could hardly wait to park my pickup on the rocky dirt road off Route 192. I started by the telephone pole that intersected the field. In spite of being lost in the experience, I noticed that there were more weeds growing throughout the field than in previous years—even some small birch, alder, and poplar bushes. I made a mental note to mention this to Shirley Guptill, from whom I had purchased the land, and who was responsible for its upkeep. I had picked several quarts of berries and had shed my shirt in response to the hot sun on my back, when a pickup slowed, turned in, and parked just back of my pickup.Thinking it to be family members who were due to join me, I had not turned to look before the car door closed and was somewhat surprised to see Shirley walking toward me. After usual friendly greetings, I mentioned the weeds in the field. He told me that he had been stopping by frequently during the last month, hoping to see me. He had been having some health problems, and had been unable to carry out the necessary management practices on the blueberry field, and that now, with the crop ready for harvesting, his regular crew of rakers had taken jobs elsewhere. Shirley apologized for not getting word to me before, but he had no other choice; he had to relinquish his agreement to take care of the blueberry field...including the current crop. Without prior warning, I was suddenly confronted with a responsibility for which I had no experience, little knowledge, and no equipment. My only commercial experience with berry picking had been when Tom Sparrow paid me one cent a quart for picking strawberries, when I was ten years-old. Now, living 260 miles away from the field, my enjoyment of and addiction to picking berries was of absolutely no help for dealing with the predicament in which I found myself. Fortunately, I did have a three week vacation from my regular position. Since owning the blueberry land, I had taken most of my vacation time in August, but the better part of it, I had spent fishing. Though son Jim and I had purchased blueberry rakes, and had learned to use them, our method was to rake particularly clean berries, to make it easier to pick them over for family use. It was far too slow a method for commercial use, and furthermore, two rakes would have been able to harvest only a small part of the field before the season ended. With available local rakers already signed up by other area growers, who would I find to rake mine? Who would buy them? These were the immediate short-term problems; there was no time to even consider the long-term ones.

2

My Addiction

Berry picking, like hunting and fishing, during my boyhood was a part of family survival, and the children, especially the boys, participated in each as soon as they were big enough. Berries meant wild and cultivated strawberries, followed by raspberries, blackberries, then blueberries and cranberries. They were eaten fresh, made into pies, puddings, muffins, jams, and jellies. They were put up in glass jars, and fall found farmers' cellar shelves lined with rows of nature's bounties. Jelly sandwiches dominated school lunch boxes, and a wide variety of berry pies and berry sauces complemented the winter holiday feasts.

I was a berry picker from earliest memory. First, wild strawberries by the cupful that my mother whipped with fresh skimmed cream to make a pink frosting. Then I received my first paycheck, by or before ten years of age, picking strawberries for a neighbor for one cent per quart...one day earning a whole dollar. I also picked strawberries from my father's commercial crop as part of my farm chores. I picked raspberries, currants, and gooseberries that we raised, which my father would sell on his weekly trips to the city.

Picking blueberries however was a family event. It may have been as early as 1921, the year Papa bought his first Model T Ford. He had probably found the burn area, not far from York Pond, when deer hunting the year before. He knew there would be berries there come August. With Uncle Charlie, Aunt Edna, and Cousin Ruth in their Model T; and with my parents, my brother and me in our own—Papa driving—we traveled about ten miles, then into York Woods, as far as the barely passable road through the woods allowed. From there we walked a short distance, carrying our picnic baskets filled with sandwiches, cake, and home-made root beer, to where the berries grew.

When we found a considerable area of lowbush blueberries, everyone set to picking from the bountiful supply. Soon my father became restless and knowing of a swampy area where highbush berries grew, he left with an empty bucket to pick the larger berries. He let me tag along with my own bucket, a two-pound lard pail. Standing barefoot in several inches of mossy water, I couldn't reach the berries, which grew far above my head on rugged bushes, which considering my size, seemed like trees. Not to be thwarted, I tied the lard pail to a string, hung it around my neck and climbed the *trees* to fill my small berry pail, while Papa filled his ten-quart galvanized water pail.

I remained at home until I was twenty-one, and was without doubt the major supplier of every wild berry to the family larder, and I enjoyed the benefits derived as the results of my mother's cooking and preserving. To this day I am addicted to berry picking.

3
My Introduction to "Blueberryland"

My own introduction to the commercial farming of Maine wild lowbush blueberries occurred in the fall of 1937. It was unintentional, and unrelated to blueberries as such, and it in no way foretold a future, closer contact with the industry. I had long been acquainted with Hay Fields, Little Field, The Backfield, The Hill Field, The Garter Field, The Ice Pond Field, and many other fields identified by various names. But that year, for the first time, I traveled over the Airline Road from Brewer to Wesley with two friends in search of one Thatcher Guptill, who, we had been told by an acquaintance of his, could find us appropriate accommodations in an area populated with big white-tailed bucks. The details of that Thanksgiving holiday period are a story for another book.

We had reached the top of Day Hill in Wesley well before dawn, and it was not until after baked beans and hot blueberry biscuits for breakfast at Thatcher's kitchen table, that we found ourselves walking behind Thatcher, who was driving his two-horse dray, with our meager camping supplies, across a hundred-acre blueberry field.

The blueberry field, opposite the one-room schoolhouse, and the faint trail through it, fell away from the higher point of Day Hill and entered the paper company-owned forest lands at a hardly discernable opening among the fir and spruce.

I will never forget that downhill, half-mile walk across the blueberry field, and the chilling north wind and the tiny snow crystals that stung our faces before we saw them, which should have warned us of the three-day blizzard that was to follow. The

5

Blueberry field on Day Hill.

storm increased as we continued for four miles on the long unused and overgrown woods road. We forded Beaver Dam Stream and came to another blueberry field, this one known locally as the Poacher's Burn. With abundant blueberries available roadside, this far away field was seldom harvested. The field somehow got burned often enough to prevent tree growth and keep the blueberry bush growth young, and consequently had become a favorite fall place for deer to feed. By the time we had reached the Poacher's Burn, the snow depth had increased to nearly cover the low short berry bushes. This was the area where Thatcher told us deer would be feeding during night and would be nearby in the thick evergreen forest during the day. It was becoming a huge, white field.

For the next fifteen years, with hunting companions, I made annual trips in November, following the horses and wagon off Day Hill and walking down over the blueberry field, through four miles of paper company forest, over the river, and across the

Poacher's Burn. During this time, I became acquainted with and made friends with many of the natives. They all being blueberry growers, many of my questions and much of our conversation included blueberries and the challenges they faced in growing them, from weather to poaching, from crop size to price paid by the processors. The big hayfields that once had grown hay to feed the logging company oxen and horses had long since been allowed to be overrun by wild lowbush blueberries. In the process, Wesley had become a blueberry town.

In early August of 1942, I took my bride of two years over the Airline Road to Wesley, as much to explain and justify my annual vacation being spent there, as in the hope that she too would enjoy the trip. We visited with my friends while there, and observed the roadside blueberry fields that extended far back to the seemingly endless forest panorama. We spent a night in a small cabin on the edge of a field just bursting with the blue of ripening berries at harvest time.

Picking from bushes just outside our cabin door, we had blueberries for breakfast, after which we walked down over the blueberry field and followed the old woods road to the river, just through the Poacher's Burn, and spent a night in the old hunting cabin on Possum Pond.

I remember Thatcher Guptill telling me then that he was paid four cents per pound by the canning factory that year, and that he paid the rakers thirty-five cents per bushel to rake them. It had been a bad year for blueberries, one of the lowest for price, but Thatcher owned at least three blueberry fields—more than a hundred acres—and with free family labor and little expense, other than taxes and paying the rakers, the wild berries provided a cash crop, and he was not complaining.

4

DESTINY

At the beginning of a November, sometime in the early 40s, I arrived at our remote hunting camp on Possum Pond and found that the top of the front sight on my Winchester 30-30 carbine had somehow been broken off. Having no spare sight with me and with many miles to walk to the nearest transportation from which I might go on to a gun shop, I attempted to compensate for the broken sight by aiming low. It proved not very accurate, and I missed hitting my target with every shot.

With a friend who also had not tagged a deer that year, I returned to Wesley during the long Thanksgiving weekend, and stayed overnight with friends on Day Hill. We spent the evening visiting John Milton Roberts (called Milt) and his wife, Muriel, who was a daughter of Thatcher Guptill.

Milt and Muriel lived in an old farmhouse on the corner of a blueberry field about two miles from Wesley corner, on the road to Machias. At the kitchen table we played cribbage, and talked about big white-tailed bucks. Frequently, Milt left the table to step outside, and before we left, he suggested that we should step outside with him, where he flashed a multi-battery flashlight onto a well-antlered buck that was feeding on the remains of Milt's garden, only a few yards from where we were standing. We resisted the urge to risk being caught by the wardens, and Milt offered to hunt with us the next morning.

Chet and I were at Milt's at dawn. After walking across Milt's garden, and down across his blueberry field, the four of us—Milt,

The author (center), Chet at right and Milt at left, tagging deer at the Airline Inn in Wesley.

my partner Chet, myself, and Muriel's younger brother, Alexander—stationed ourselves, in that order, along a woods road that divided the blueberry field and extended into the woodlands beyond. A crust, too shallow not to break when walking on it, had, after several days of warm weather, frozen over the foot of snow on the ground. It made any attempt to progress into the woodland noisy enough that any deer within a mile would be warned of our presence.

Only a short distance into the woods, I stood quietly, listening to Alex, off to my left, and Chet and Milt, off to my right, as they crashed through the crust. I stood for some time, and then heard what sounded like deer. Having heard our footsteps, they were making moves to avoid our seeing them. Familiar with the tactics of a doe with mature fawns, I thought that they might just stop in a thicket and let the noisy hunters pass on each side, then retreat back from where they had moved. They did, and in their retreat, the three deer came crashing straight towards me, one so close that

I could have reached out and touched it. We suddenly had three deer, and when we had dragged them out to the nearby road, Milt went to purchase a license so that all three could be tagged. Though venison was frequently on his table, Milt had not purchased a hunting license all those years. Young Alex must have heard the shots, but he continued trekking through the crusted snow and eventually reached the Airline Road, and then home, before dark.

During the next twelve years, I continued the annual hunting trips and summer visits to Wesley. I made acquaintances and friends among the residents of Day Hill, and became familiar with the unbroken terrain of blueberry fields that dominated the landscape both sides of Route 9 over the hill. Most of the residents were born in the homes in which they lived; many were third or fourth generation of the original settlers.

The cellar hole and well still remain on the spot where Milt and Muriel's old house stood. Blueberries grow where the buck had fed in Milt's garden. The woods road still divides the blueberry field at a low place from which the field rises in both directions. During that brief and exciting visit to Wesley, I certainly never imagined that I would eventually come to own that land. The fir trees I was among when I shot the deer, would mature, be killed by an infestation of spruce bud worm, and I would cut them. I never dreamed that I would own that blueberry field back of the garden where we saw the big buck, that I would mow and burn that field, and that I would kneel on every inch of that field while raking the blueberries that grew there.

5

BALDFACE

I considered myself fairly impartial as to which berry I preferred to pick, only waiting impatiently for each kind to ripen in season, but for some reason, the lowbush blueberries seemed more seductive than the strawberries, raspberries, or blackberries. Perhaps it was because they remained wild and untamed, unlike other previously wild berries that had become cultivated. I did seem more likely to let picking wild blueberries delay, or interfere with a fishing trip, than if I were picking cultivated strawberries. I am reminded of the early September weekend I took three of my teenage sons to trout fish the Lovewell River.

Some distance along the river, which paralleled a dirt road as it wound up into the Ossipee Mountains, with no trout, we detoured to a small pond in search of better luck. The fish did not bite there either, but many of the nearby or taller bushed plants along the shore were heavy with blueberries. With rods under our arms, and knee deep in the water, we were soon filling our creels with blueberries. As we picked, a man and a boy suddenly separated the bushes from the land side and greeted us. They had come over the mountain from where they lived in Ossipee. He introduced himself as Walter Kimball; the boy was his son. He had been checking out patches of wild ginseng. Mr. Kimball was a mountain man, that is, he pretty much lived off the land, digging and selling ginseng, and other wild roots, picking wild berries, fishing the lakes and streams, trapping, and hunting.

Seeing us with creels full of blueberries, he reminded us of how much sweeter and better the lowbush berries were, and he

Mountain cranberries.

asked if we had ever been up to Baldface for them. We had not. He told us that the frost had already destroyed the berries on Baldface, but that if we would like to go there another year, he would be glad to let us know a few days before he went, and we could go with him. Baldface is a small mountain located northeast of Conway, New Hampshire in the town of Chatham, near the Maine border.

True to his word, Mr. Kimball called the last week in August the next year, and we arranged to meet him at the end of a dirt road where we would take the Slippery Brook Trail. He was waiting when we arrived soon after daybreak of the assigned morning. He led the way, and three of my sons and I followed with light backpacks filled with containers for the berries. I had always considered myself a good walker, but Mr. Kimball, with long legs and long steps, glided over the rough rock trail at a speed I found difficult to maintain. It was more than an hour before he stopped by the stream, bent to get a drink of water, and suggested we fill our canteens - as we were leaving the brook, and would not be near water again until we returned later in the day. It was not a rest period. He led us off on a long steep climb, and never stopped until we were above the tree line, and in the midst of patches of ripe thick lowbush blueberries. With time out for lunch, we filled our containers with berries in plenty of time to return to our car before dark.

I learned two things that day. First, during lunch, as we drank from our canteens, he took a cucumber from his pack. It was not only food, he explained, but also his supply of water. One or more cucumbers replaced canteens for us on many hikes in following years. Second, as well as blueberries on Baldface, there were many small cranberries, and we picked some of them too. He called them *mountain cranberries*, but on the Maine coast, they are often called *island cranberries*. Yielding but one or two berries about the size of the blueberries we were picking, on a two-inch tall bush, they were slow to pick. But the flavor and rich red color of the cooked sauce so surpassed that of the common, or bog cranberry, that in later years, we made annual trips to Baldface just to get the cranberries.

They are called *fox berries* in Nova Scotia, where they were once shipped in barrels by steamships to Boston. On annual trips to Nova Scotia, when visiting friends there, I picked them along the rocky shore near my friend's house (the friend always picking faster than I could). For many years, I picked these mountain cranberries (or fox berries) in Nova Scotia, rather than make the long five-mile hike, or shorter, but steeper, route up Baldface. In Newfoundland, another near cousin of blueberries is the partridgeberry, actually a lingenberry, a sub-arctic berry that grows in northern areas around the world, and on the mountaintops, on rocky islands, and by the coast of New England

I distinctly remember one trip up Baldface that included my wife and several of our children. Hot dogs were a part of our lunch, and in the process of cutting sticks on which to cook the hot dogs over a campfire, I carelessly mishandled my jackknife and cut a considerable gash in my wrist. With tourniquet bandages made from the back and tail of my shirt, we stopped the bleeding, partook of our hot dog rolls, cookies, and cucumbers, and continued picking berries until time to make it back over the steep, downhill, five mile trail, to our car before dark. Disinfectants and seven stitches by a doctor at the hospital emergency room assured a safe and rapid recovery.

We made annual trips over a period of more than twenty years to Baldface for blueberries, until I purchased Shirley Guptill's blueberry field. Son Jim has persisted to hike Baldface each year, sometimes camping on top overnight in order to replenish his supply, never missing a year since that first trip in about 1955.

6

BLUEBERRY TRAIL

Even I find a measure of confusion in the story of how I unknowingly wove the circumstances that resulted in my being the owner of—and responsible for—land that included as much as twenty acres of lowbush blueberries.

After being employed as a poultry health researcher for twenty-eight years, I retired at age sixty-five, purchased a bulldozer, and spent the following fifteen years leisurely building roads, while cutting and marketing logs from my own woodland. However, it was my avocations, hunting and fishing, both before and after, as well as during those years that inadvertently led to my tending that blueberry field.

The annual hunting trips that began in 1937, and the added fishing trips during the 1970s that came by way of the friends made in the Wesley area, included many hours of blueberry talk, because that was their lives. Joined to them because of the common experience of being a farm boy, a berry picker, a hunter and fisherman, and a lover of the land and forests, I gradually became familiar with the history of the local families, and with it the history of the blueberry industry.

Step by step, from that cold day in November, 1937, when I walked across a blueberry field, the intrigue of the Poacher's Burn, evidence of my attraction to the land and town when I brought my young wife there, and a broken rifle sight, led me to the land I would own. Even then, I purchased the hundred acres of land that, covered mostly by pine, spruce, fir, and cedar, was a haven for wild life, without consideration of the twenty-acre field of blueberry bushes. My wildest dreams did not include interference to a fishing trip by the rude awakening of being responsible for a crop of blueberries ready to be harvested, and for which I was not prepared, or equipped, to rake or market.

Looking back, the trail is reasonably clear, but it was not planned. It was not intentional. It just happened.

7

ENTREPRENEUR

In 1952, after fifteen years of annual, and successful deer hunting trips to Wesley, I bought a farm in the foothills of the White Mountains in New Hampshire where deer were plentiful. My young family expanded to four sons and three daughters, and claimed more of my time. It was not until 1972 that hunting deer, not blueberries, brought me back to a rented camp in Wesley. I had kept contact during the years, when passing through on the Airline Road while visiting friends or for business reasons during trips to Canada. Thatcher Guptill had passed away and the house and barn where I had first met him had burned. His son, Shirley, had built a small house and the hunting camp where I stayed, next to the burned-out cellar hole. During our week of hunting, and the increased number of visits during the months that followed, old acquaintances became close friends. The next spring, when my son Russ, returned from a three-year stint with the Peace Corps in India, and indicated an interest in sharing the cost of building a hunting camp in the area, I spread the word that I was looking for land suitable for the purpose.

Shirley Guptill promptly told me that because of his poor health, he would sell me the hundred-acre lot he had inherited from his father. It was located a mile or so off the Airline Road, on the highway to Machias. I was interested, but he wanted to delay the sale for a year or two until he retired from service with the state highway department. The lot was mostly forested, but about twenty acres, facing the highway, had been one of his father's blueberry fields.

The author's blueberry field in Wesley covered with hay bales.

Carl Day, who, with his big double horse team, had transported our hunting party the five miles back into the paper company
land to South Beaver Dam Lake after Thatcher had died, had sold
his farm in Wesley and moved to land left to him on Nineteen
Road, just off the Airline Road, at the top of Sally Hill in the next
town of Crawford. My cousin, and some of his hunting friends,
had previously bought land there from Carl for a camp. Carl
worked on the state highway crew with Shirley, and soon learned
of my interest in land for a camp. We met. He made an offer for a
two-acre lot, and my son Russ and I agreed to buy it. Russ and I,
and friends, set a date later in August when we would gather there
and build a camp.

Word reached Shirley of my purchase and he promptly came
to see me. He was then willing to sell his hundred acres without
waiting until he retired. This time, Shirley extolled the added
value of the blueberry land and insisted I go with him to see it. A
big crop of berries was beginning to ripen as we walked across the
field and I tried hard to hide the influence of my berry picking

Rakers in the field opposite the author's.

addiction. Knowing so little about the commercial aspects of low-bush blueberry production, and that it would be another six years before I retired and had time to work the field, I agreed that, except for letting me and my family harvest what we wanted for personal use, he would maintain and harvest blueberries as long as he was physically able. He also requested that I spread the payments over a three-year period for tax reasons. Shirley delivered the deed and I was the owner of a blueberry field and an entrepreneur in the blueberry business.

Few changes had taken place in the production of blueberries from the time of the first shipments to factories nearly a hundred years before. They were now spraying some fields to control the blueberry fruit fly. The mechanical winnowers had come into use, and shipping boxes, though still made of wood, were being filled from the wide side to accommodate the winnower. Roads and the trucks that hauled the berries to market had improved, and the open boxes were transported without covers, stacked high and tight, on the trucks.

The author's camp in Crawford.

My participation in management of the blueberry field operation had been purposely delayed by the deal to have Shirley continue as long as he was able. But soon my son Jim, and I, plus a flood of family, friends, and visitors, took advantage of harvesting free berries according to my agreement. We purchased blueberry rakes. We fished a nearby lake a while in the morning, until the fog and dew had dried off, then we went to the field and, carefully, slowly learning how to rake, we harvested a dozen or more quarts before lunch. We enjoyed a brief rest after lunch, then spent until dark fishing another lake, and evening picking over the berries. When our freezer was full, we gave quart baskets filled with the berries to anyone we knew who could use them.

.We watched the rakers in a field across the road from mine, and on and over the hill in a field abutting mine to the north. Seeing them, age ten to seventy, swinging rakes day after day, and the piles of half-bushel boxes full of berries collected by trucks each night, it seemed that there was no great training required or effort put forth by those involved. We soon learned that, like hoeing corn, cutting a leaning tree, even driving a car, raking blue-

The author in the stern of the boat with daughter-in-law Trish and son Dan Staples.

berries did not require perfection, and few rakers attained it or even attempted to.

Jim and I, however, raking relatively small amounts for personal use or to give away, spent considerable time learning how to manipulate the rakes in such a way that the berries would be picked clean of the bushes and most grass, leaves, and weeds, without jamming. This did of course slow production, and the method, which is used when, raking berries for fresh-pack, would be hardly profitable for the commercial rakers.

In 1975, a sixteen foot used house trailer became available near my home for a reasonable price. I bought it, hauled it to Wesley, and placed it by an old camp (and outhouse) near the highway and midway of the field. It would, I reasoned, provide shade during the heat of the day for those picking berries, provide overnight sleeping accommodation for visitors, and a nearby place to keep dry during a thundershower.

We became so involved in the pleasures of our addiction, blueberries and fishing, and being able to provide good picking to relatives and friends, I hardly noticed that Shirley raked fewer and fewer each year, that though we could always find an area where the berries were plentiful, other areas had been over-run with grass and weeds, birch and poplar trees growing undisturbed, wild cherry and wild roses covering patches where we had picked berries in past years. Spring burning had occurred haphazardly in relatively small areas. No mowing had been done.

The north part of the field had been burned in the spring of 1977. That was when Shirley told me he was no longer able to properly take care of the blueberry land, that he wanted to be released of his responsibilities of the agreement, that it would be mine from that time on.

I had expected Shirley to continue up-keep on the blueberry land another two years, at least until I retired. I was caught completely unprepared, without adequate knowledge of the industry, without adequate equipment, and without time to adequately prepare to rake and market what appeared to be a reasonably good crop beginning to ripen.

It was time I learned more about the blueberry industry, its history, and management practices. To whom should I turn first to find a market for my berries, to hire rakers for a crop waiting to be harvested?

PART II: MAINE WILD LOWBUSH BLUEBERRIES

A bunch of white blueberries.

8

MAINE WILD

I learned that blueberry bushes are botanically classified belonging to the genus *vaccinium*, which is in the *ericaceae* family of plants. Blueberry bushes belong to the heath family of plants that grow throughout the northern hemisphere. Blueberries vary in color from white to blue to red and black. Like its close relative the cranberry (also known as the *bog berry, fox berry, mountain* or *island cranberry),* and *lingenberry (partridge berry, and cow berry)*, the blueberry has many names, including *huckleberry, whortleberry, bilberry,* and *attitash* (the native Indian name). Blueberries grow on bushes varying in height from a few inches to eight feet or more.

The highbush variety of blueberry has been cultivated for commercial production, but there are relatively few highbush farms in Maine. Some of the highbush farms use natural wild berries, and others, the cultivated strains. Mostly, they offer pick your own harvesting, and yield little commercial volume when compared with lowbush production. Highbush berries are grown and are of commercial importance in other states, including Michigan, New Jersey, and North Carolina.

Three species of the lowbush variety are native to Maine. One of these species tends to dominate, but in most fields, small patches of other species that vary noticeably in bush size, color of fruit and leaves, and leaf structure can be found.

The most productive, natural, blueberry areas appear to have done well on what was considered poor land, that is on natural eskers of sandy, gravelly, hilly soil, with little shade, free of tree growth and other competition. However, this may be misleading, because higher yields follow new plant growth, and such growth will follow a fire that has pruned the old growth, producing large areas of open space and new growth simultaneously. Because of grass and shrub growth, these open areas become more susceptible to natural as well as set fires, promoting the probability of repeated burnings over a period of many hundreds, if not thousands of years. It had been found advantageous to fertilize the older fields to maintain soil quality, and the commercial growing areas have extended well into areas with better soil quality than that of the barrens.

Blueberry bushes can be found most everywhere in Maine, in fact, throughout New England. Following a forest fire, they appear promptly with the first new growth of vegetation. Two and more years after new road construction, we see cars parked alongside and pickers on the cleared banks. The treeless right-of-ways beneath power lines are favorite areas for those who like to pick blueberries.

From underground rhyzomes that must have survived from previous growth in the area, or from seeds that have passed through the digestive tract of a bird or animal, blueberry bushes, spread in all directions. Bushes observed on the floor of forested areas tend to be thin and scraggly. Of the few berries that they produce, the ones that ripen are quickly eaten by birds.

In the spring, the lowbush plants, often with blossoms, wet the feet and legs of hikers on mountain trails. At higher elevations, most of the blooms are killed by frost before they can fruit, and of the few berries that ripen, most are picked and eaten by the hikers. Finding suitable habitats above or below tree line, the blueberry bush, like its cousin the cranberry, survives unobserved until its berries ripen.

The variables that have influenced commercial blueberry production in Maine over the years include items as diverse as transportation, edible product preservation, soil type, and air drainage (effecting temperature). A band of rolling hills and eskers with sandy or gravely soils, twenty miles inland and extending the entire coastline of Maine—with the nearby ocean stabilizing temperature to some extent—is the area most favorable to blueberry production. Few other agricultural products compete. A canning factory in Maine was the first in the nation, apparently in the world, to can and sell blueberries. From that first commercial effort there has been a steady increase in blueberry production and distribution, with sales worldwide.

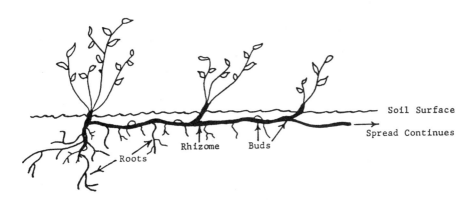

Lowbush blueberry plants grow from seed. These plants send out underground stems called rhizomes. The rhizomes burrow near the surface, periodically sending out new stems. Roots are established on the rhizomes as they grow.

From *Blueberry Information Guide*

9

HISTORY

The beginning of the Maine wild lowbush blueberry as a viable food source may well have occurred many centuries ago on the so-called barrens of what is now Washington and Hancock Counties. Black bears, sitting comfortably in the midst of a heavily fruited patch of aromatic berries, would crudely gather the fruit from the lowbush plants to open mouths with long sweeps of their clawed forefeet. The ever-alert white-tailed deer, ears sweeping every direction for danger signals, daintily nibbling a generous cluster, would hold their heads high, alert, before taking another step or two, to bend again for another small helping of sweet, ripe, berries. Blackbirds, grosbeaks, perhaps now extinct carrier pigeons, after resting briefly in nearby tall trees to check the area for security, would sweep down in massive flocks to feast on the bountiful harvest.

Before the white settlement of the barrens area, the local native Indians had long known of, and utilized, the wild blueberry crops. They undoubtedly observed that better crops occurred the second year following a natural or accidental burn, and they set fires on areas of older bushes with poor crops. Like the assembling of families and tribes to the rivers at spawning time for salmon, perch, and alewives, they also swarmed to the barrens to harvest, eat, and dry the wild blueberries.

The first recorded ownership of the land, by way of grants, was made to favored individuals of the ruling English monarch, some of whom never crossed the Atlantic to personally see their property. They maintained ownership by convincing others to settle, by way of offering ownership to specific areas, sub-grants as it were, and often these land barons paid little attention to anything other than the fishing and timber resources of their property. There was no possible income from the inland barrens, and they essentially ignored such areas, if they even knew about them.

Living conditions in the area, before the War of Independence, are described in *The History of Columbia*, published by the Columbia Historical Society, which includes the copy of a petition by the settlers to the colonial government in Boston. Maine remained a part of Massachusetts until 1820.

The petition in part reads:

...and neither law nor gospel embraced among us, every one doing what's right in his own eyes, and a great spirit of mobbing and rioting prevails. Cursing, swearing, fighting, threatening, stealing, pulling down houses and the like as we can't sleep at nights without fear and living such a distance from any authority that we labor under a great disadvantage of obtaining relief in such matters....

The signers of this petition are listed below, many of whom still have descendants today in Columbia and Columbia Falls: Moses Plummer, Samuel Drisko, William Mitchell, Benjamin Look, Chase Stevens, Edward Cates, Seth Norton, Samuel Knowls, John Hall, Isiah Nash, Samuel Coffing, Joseph Drisko Jr., Nathl Buck, John Drisko (his mark), Daniel Look, Owen McKensey, Edmund Stevens, George Tinney, James Nash, Joseph, Isaac Smith, Robin Groas, Noah Mitchell, Samuel Nash, Joseph Mitchell, Ebenezer Coal, James Bryant, William Hix, Thomas, Joseph Tebbut, Samuel, Joseph Nash, Jr.

In 1779, their ports blocked by British ships, and near starvation, the settlers again petitioned the General Court of Massachusetts for assistance saying, "Some of us want for bread." The government in Boston sent some supplies, but was unable to send enough for all. The British tried to win back these settlers to little avail. "Our people were strong, and none turned against the new homeland." They struggled and finally won, never realizing that they were ultimately helping to determine the boundary line of the State of Maine and the United States as well. If the eastern parts of Maine had fallen to the British, this area would undoubtedly today be a part of Canada.

As settlements spread from the ocean-front harbors and navigable rivers to the interior, berry picking, like hunting and fishing, became an integral part of living off the land, and pioneer families in the area joined the native Indians, as well as the bears, deer, and birds on the annual pilgrimage to harvest blueberries from the barrens. It retained its status as common land, rather than anyone claiming it as private property.

The native Indians had long since learned to dehydrate blueberries through exposure to sunlight or by using an outside fire, thus making it possible to store large quantities of berries as an addition to their winter food supply. They beat the dry berries to a powder and mixed the powder with parched meal to make a delicious dish, which they called *sautauthig*. Many rubbed it into their venison pemmican to help preserve the meat longer. They bartered large quantities of the dried berries in baskets to captains of coastal fishing boats, and later to the English settlers and ship captains that serviced the deep harbor villages between Boston and Bangor, and east to Calais and Halifax.

The first record of an actual sale of fresh-picked berries was in 1860: forty bushels per day, picked fresh from the Epping plains, packed in round wooden one or two quart boxes, which were crated, then transported to Rockland and Bangor by stagecoach, or brought by horse and wagon from the barrens to the nearest harbor, which would have been Millbridge, some ten miles away or Jonesboro. Then they would be taken by coastal boat to market.

It may be assumed that, whether the berries were dried or fresh, the settlers had previously shipped them on coastal vessels to relatives and friends living in cities to the south, such as Portsmouth and Boston. Fresh picked blueberries, unlike other native berries, such as strawberries, blackberries and raspberries, remain firm and wholesome for a week or more despite handling and fluctuations in temperature.

The barrens remained a free and open area for picking blueberries by all who chose to go there for a hundred years after the English had first settled the area.

10

The First Canned Blueberries

During the Civil War, in the 1860s, several companies began canning fish and lobsters to meet the increasing food demands of the Union armies. A group in Cherryfield made crude attempts to can blueberries. The berries were cooked in an open pan over a brick oven fire. Much of the product spoiled, but the method was improved, and they, along with other canning companies located in Millbridge, Cherryfield, Columbia Falls, Harrington, and Machias, canned blueberries during the harvest season. That the fish factory in Machias was reported to be canning blueberries indicated that berries were being harvested farther down the coast than the barrens, though the fresh berries may have been hauled by horses and wagons the twenty-five miles from the Epping plains to Machias, or even transported by ship, from the ports at Addison, Harrington, or Millbridge.

Though lasting only as long as the month-long harvest season, and mostly limited to harvest areas within horse and wagon distance from the cannery, this market was of commercial importance to both those who picked the berries, as well as those who owned and worked in the canning factory. Trade by the settlers was mostly by way of barter, as cash was a rare item for those who lived outside a settlement. Picking berries had become an occupation in which every member of the family, ten years of age or older, could participate. That could bring in fifteen dollars a day for the family in cash, a tidy sum back when men were being paid fifty cents for a day's work. This resulted not only in a sharp

An early Maine blueberry canning company.

increase in the number of pickers, but also resulted in the barrens area experiencing more fires—undoubtedly set by pickers. This increased acreage came at the expense of the adjoining forests. At some point, the pickers, most likely meeting in tents during a stormy day, reached the conclusion that because the berries were free, the canning factories could afford a penny raise in the price for berries delivered from two and a half cents to three cents per quart. The factories, with one exception, refused, and the berry pickers went out on a strike, which was quickly settled to their advantage.

It was inevitable that with so much cash being generated from what was originally considered wasteland, and to offset the burning of the valuable timber caused by expansion of the blueberry land, that the land owners would at some point feel they were entitled to a share of the harvest.

In 1871, William Freeman of Cherryfield first posted his land,

A sampling of Maine canned blueberry companies.

requiring that all berry pickers submit to a contract that would entitle him to one-half cent for each quart picked. His no trespass signs were disregarded or used for campfire wood. Mr. Freeman, a lawyer, representing his own interests as well as that of other owners, totaling 70,000 acres of the barrens, then requested that the canning factories would pay them. One factory resisted, and Freeman sued. He won his case in the Superior Court of Maine after a bitter five-year battle, and the barrens were no longer regarded as common land where blueberries could be picked without payment. The canning factories contracted with the landowners to have their own representatives arrange for burning the fields, cutting brush, picking the berries, and shipping them from designated areas. This arrangement, with some modification, has continued to the present time.

The History of Columbia gives an accounting of the first mills built in the area:

> In 1881 a canning factory was established at the site of the Crandon Shipyard, known as the Columbia Falls Packing Co. It was followed by another on the western side of the river below the bridge and was operated by Joseph Coffin. It burned in the early 1900's and was rebuilt in front of the railroad station. . . . The mill lasted a few years and was transformed into a packing plant by Hall and later became the Pleasant River Canning Co. Jasper Wyman once leased the factory at the Columbia Railroad Station, owned by Bill Hathaway, from a Portland concern. It was changed from blueberry canning to string beans by Hathaway and was finally a freezing plant for fish....

11

TO TAME

While lowbush blueberries were commercially canned in fish canning factories in Maine no earlier than the 1860s, they were probably sold as fresh before then. Highbush blueberries were undoubtedly domesticated before the commercial use of lowbush berries. It is probable that settlers had transplanted selected wild bushes in their gardens, if that could be called domesticated. This made them more accessible, and less susceptible to bird and bear predation. Though wild highbush berries growing in swampy areas were native to Maine and other New England states, they remained of small commercial importance, because of the competition from the free wild lowbush berries, which were far more plentiful and concentrated. The highbush berries are of considerable commercial importance in New Jersey, and are now grown in other states, providing competition for Maine's fresh picked berries. The selected highbush plants produce larger berries than the lowbush variety, and are not as sweet. They reach the markets months before the Maine crop is harvested.

Though hardly a taming process, William Freeman's successful suit to prevent free access to the barrens amounted at least to a fence, which corralled some acres of the species. The fence was more effective in keeping pickers out than in keeping berry production isolated to the barrens. In fact, like requiring a license to hunt wild game, and to catch freshwater fish, it limited the legal picking of wild berries on the barrens to those who paid for the privilege. And, if it didn't result in the actual taming of wild blueberries, it did set in motion a process that still continues, which not so much tamed the lowbush berries, but rather captured and enslaved them.

Burning the blueberry fields was the natural method of pruning the bushes. Like cutting off, or otherwise removing old growth, it prompted new growth which while fruitless the following year, resulted in increased production in the second year. Burning became more important after the introduction of the blueberry rake, because the rake's wire tines (like those of a comb) were more apt to be caught in the stiff old growth, making it more difficult to push the rake through without jamming the berries and sometimes uprooting the bush.

Again, from *The History of Columbia*:

As early as 1883 Abuja W. Tabbut was making all-metal blueberry rakes. These replaced the crude wood and wire device that some individuals had made for their own use. The number made each year increased until 1910 when 300 rakes per year was the average. Only two important changes have occurred in the design. About 1900 or slightly earlier the shape of the rake was changed to a flat bottom followed a few years later by reversing the handle from outside to inside and over the teeth. This change made them easier on the wrist when in use, and led to the demand for larger or wider rakes. In April 1918, because of ill health, Tabbut turned the business over to his grandson, Clarence Drisko. The manufacture of rakes has been carried on to the present time, 1976, with an annual output of about 2000 per year.

12

DURING *100* YEARS

There were few changes in the production and processing of blueberries during the one hundred years since its commercial beginning when William Freeman posted no trespassing signs on his barrens property.

The lobster and fish canning factories contracted with and paid the landowner. At the start, they arranged with local workers to burn the fields on a three-year rotation, hire pickers, and have the berries transported to the factories. They purchased directly from the smaller landowners, and from individuals who still found free berries to pick. They, and larger local storeowners purchased the early ripening berries and sold them fresh in one-quart round wooden boxes. In 1898 there were about 30,000 cases of twenty-four cans each, canned by the factories. It amounted to half the crop. The rest, about 38,000 bushels, were sold as fresh berries.

The coastal railroad was completed in 1898, expanding the marketing range for both fresh and canned berries. Canning factories along the coast in Harrington, Columbia Falls, and Machias began canning blueberries in season, indicating—considering that local transportation consisted of horse and wagon—berries were being grown east of the barrens. These new fields were found to produce large crops of better quality berries than on the barrens where fires over as long a period as centuries had depleted the humus and drained the soil of nutrients. As stated earlier, pastures and fields on old farms needed during the logging days no longer needed to produce hay for horses once used in the woods. Some of the fields had already reverted to growing wild lowbush

Coop members Bill and Nellie Hayward. Knapp photo, courtesy of the Haywards.

blueberry bushes, offering a new opportunity to support families in an area where work was not plentiful.

Factory canning of blueberries persisted as a seasonal by-product of lobster and fish processing and canning, much of the same equipment being adapted for blueberries. Mostly hand work was involved in preparing the product. The berries were picked over by hand, then cooked while being forced through a long tube by a screw-auger contraption that passed through a heated chamber. The berries were then hand dipped into the cans before being capped.

In 1921, following World War I, the berry market became severely depressed. The pitifully low prices offered by the canning companies resulted in four marketing cooperatives being formed by the larger growers. The coops that year canned 67,000 bushels, a third of the total of the Washington county crop, which itself was substantially less than the year before and only three times what it had been twenty-five years earlier (80,000 bushels in 1898) when the industry was in its infancy.

History repeated itself half a century later (1979), when a period of poor prices for blueberries resulted in a number of Washington County growers becoming organized under the mantle of the National Farmers Organization (NFO), but the group did not find the NFO helpful, and after a few years, organized their own coop, Down East Blueberry Coop (DEBCO), which is still active. Members supply their own boxes and trucking, and their gross product is put out to bid, or contracted previous to raking, with a processor.

Undoubtedly, because of the convenience of the Guptill Farms processing plant in Wesley, with which many growers contract, and because so many of the fields are now owned by Guptill, few of the local growers have joined the coop. However, Joline Thornton of nearby Crawford, secretary of the organization, reports it is at present very active in nearby towns.

The growers' misery continued the following year in 1922. The blueberry fruit fly was not new to the industry, but 1922 was an especially good year for the insects. They laid their eggs in a high percentage of berries in most fields. The maggots hatched and went to market in large numbers inside the berries. Somewhere, someone found one of the little white creatures in a blueberry pie, and had it identified. The word got out. Everyone was soon looking for them in their cans of blueberries, and they found them. The U.S. department of Agriculture and the National Canners Association got involved. Fresh berries were banned at state lines, and sales of canned berries declined.

The canneries developed a sample test for berries brought to their unloading platforms. A representative sample of berries was scooped from the top of the box, poured into a glass jar of water, and shaken. A standard was set for an acceptable number of maggots in a specific number of samples before the berries would be accepted. Growers accused the factories of determining acceptance or rejection on the basis of the factory need, which may have been true in some circumstances.

The fruit fly was a catastrophe big enough that it resulted in growers, buyers, canning factory owners, and rakers agreeing to meet with the state extension service. The problem was serious enough that the County, state, and federal representatives all became involved. It began with crop inspections and research, and extended over a period of time. The results included acceptance of dusting the field with an insecticide during the egg laying period of the fly and the purchase of land for building research facilities for blueberries, which proved to be very effective.

Limited freezing of blueberries began as early as 1928, but had reached only 25,000 bushels, less than eight percent of the crop, by 1941. There now were 500 farms producing blueberries, less than half coming from the barrens. But there would be other problems ahead. A crop failure in 1944 resulted in a decrease in the harvested crop from 17 million pounds in 1943 to a mere 3.5 million in 1944. Again, the state was called upon for help, and it was provided. Black army cutworms were identified as the major problem and control measures were determined and put into practice.

That the state should build and operate a blueberry research farm was a major research decision of the appointed study committee resulting from the fruit fly invasion. Dean Deering, at the University of Maine in Orono, insisted on prompt and complete publicity as the plan was implemented, undoubtedly bringing a closer working relationship among the various industry participants. After due deliberation, land was purchased on Route 1 in Jonesboro, and appropriate facilities built.

Named *Blueberry Hill*, after a much-publicized contest among school children, the state blueberry research station became, and continues to be a major assistance and support to the industry.

With blueberry production expanding to all coastal counties, and some inland as well, and with competition developing from other states and Canadian provinces, Maine continued to increase production from seven million pounds in 1924, to an average of over twenty million pounds, thirty years later in 1954 (figure is a three year average).

Maine Wild Blueberry Cooperatives

Company	Contact	Telephone
DEBCO Cooperative	Walt Getchell	(207) 255-4883

Foggy Bottom Cooperative
    HCR 69, Box 42A
    East Machias, ME 04630
	Mike Look	(207) 255-4167

Knox County Blueberries
    367 Buzzell Hill Road
    Hope, ME 04847-3501
	Richard & Gwen Brodis (207) 785-4433	

Pleasant River Canning Company P.O. Box 277 Columbia, ME 04623	Merton Allen	(207) 483-4614
Sunrise Country Wild Blueberry Association, Inc. Cherryfield, ME 04622	Sanford Kelly P.O. Box 284	(207) 497-2846

13

Blueberry Hill Farm

This chapter is copied from a speech made by Maine historian Clarence A. Day at the 1959 annual Farm and Home meeting at the University of Maine at Orono and was provided by the Maine Extension Service.

Clarence A. Day's Speech

The blueberry industry has profited more than once by the way it has met an emergency. The emergency of the twenties was eliminated through research and extension work, in the control of the blueberry fly. The emergency of the forties united the industry in the successful attempt to secure the establishment of the first experimental farm in the United States devoted to research with lowbush blueberries. Both have brought lasting benefits to the industry.

Receipts from blueberries used for processing more than doubled during World War II over those of the similar period just preceding that conflict. That was in spite of the fact that yields were low in certain areas and that the crop of 1944 was a near failure – down from an estimated yield of 17,395,000 pounds processed in 1943 to 3,503,000 pounds in 1944. This, the smallest crop in more than twenty years, seemed to be the result in part of unusual weather conditions and in part to the worst outbreak of black army cut worms that the "blueberry belt" along the coast, had ever experienced.

But was that all? Why did the leaves sometimes drop off the plants before the berries were grown? Why were the berries sometimes few after an abundant bloom? How could weed plants in

Blueberry Hill Farm office. Photo by Natalie Peterson.

blueberry fields be controlled? Could anything be done to prevent winter injury? Were the fields of the farmers running out as well as the barrens? Would fertilization help? And above all could crop failure come again? It could and it did – the very next year, when the crop was not much more than half as large as that of 1943. Moreover stiff competition was developing beyond the borders of the state. New Jersey was growing as many berries (cultivated) as Washington County, and millions of pounds were being imported from Canada, some of them to be canned in factories Down East. Industry problems were now state wide.

Faced with these problems that formerly did not exist or went unrecognized, men with foresight began to seek solutions. Naturally, they turned to the University of Maine, which through its Experiment Station and Extension Service had helped so effectively in previous years. There they contacted the Dean of Agriculture, Arthur L. Deering, who at once undertook the task of persuading the various interests concerned to work together for the common good. That was no easy task. Except for a brief time in Washington County they had never worked together before. Moreover conflicts, jealousies, and animosities had grown up over the years, especially between the cooperatives and some of the privately owned concerns.

Eventually, December 5, 1944, a meeting was held at Ellsworth at which representatives of all groups and all sections were present. Attending also were the Experiment Station, the Maine Commissioner of Agriculture, and interested members of the Maine Legislature that would soon be in session.

Out of this meeting came two decisions that required legislative action. First, it was decided that the industry needed an experimental farm where the station could study these pressing problems and find solutions; and second, that the industry should tax itself to provide funds for research and increased extension work. Here the blueberry men had the precedents of the potato growers who had secured the establishment of Aroostook Farm and had agreed to an industry tax for research and the promotion of their commodity.

Buying Blueberry Hill Farm

An action committee was also appointed to attain these objectives. Members of this committee were all prominent growers and also connected with the processing section of the industry. They represented both cooperatives and private concerns and all sections of the blueberry belt. They were: Russell Mace, of Aurora, chairman; Fred C. Black, or Rockland, secretary; Roy Allen, of Sedgwick; Cole Bridges, of Calais; Henry Kontio, of West Rockport; George F. Marston, of Jonesboro; and Charles Stewart, of Cherryfield. They deserve their full measure of credit for their successful work. Two bills were introduced in the Legislature, one by Sen. Frank P. Washburn, of Washington County, to provide funds for the purchase of the farm and its equipment; and the other by Rep. Lewis H. Lackee, of Addison, to provide for an industry tax of 1 1/4 mills "per pound of fresh fruit on all blueberries grown, purchased, sold, handled or processed in this state." The tax was to be paid by the processor or shipper, who would deduct the amount from the purchase bill. Both bills became law.

Then came the task of finding a farm that would be adapted to research, well carpeted with blueberry plants, easy of access, and within the designated price range. The committee examined a large number of farms and finally selected one on Highway Route 1 in the town of Jonesboro, about halfway between the villages of Jonesboro and Columbia Falls, and in a large area of highly productive blueberry land. There were no buildings, but that instead of being a drawback, permitted the erection of a laboratory and a dwelling house well adapted to the needs of a research farm.

From the beginning, Dean Deering had insisted on keeping the public informed on the progress of the project. News stories and special articles were contributed to the press, numerous meetings were held in blueberry sections, circular letters were sent to growers. Now came the naming of the farm. A contest was conducted among 4-H club members and pupils in grade and secondary schools. More than a thousand young people proposed names; twenty-two suggested the name that was chosen – Blueberry Hill Farm. Washington County young people submitted 752 names in the contest.

The committee named to purchase the farm was now made permanent. Its new duty was to advise the authorities at the University of Maine on projects in research and extension to be financed from the proceeds of the blueberry industry tax. This committee, which changes somewhat in personnel each year, and receives no monetary reward, has rendered valuable service both to the industry and the university.

Some Results From Extension And Research

Research was begun at Blueberry Hill Farm in 1946 along these lines: Studies with fertilizers and mulches, plant breeding and propagation, and disease, insect, and weed control. Other research conducted since then has included irrigation, pruning, handling, and processing. Results in research come slowly, but already Blueberry Hill Farm has a gratifying number to its credit that are in more or less general use. They include a high quality blueberry pie filler of which 25,000 to 30,000 cases are marketed annually, the growing use of powered oil burners that can be employed for pruning in late fall as well as early spring, use of honey bees for pollination, and improved dusts to control such insects as the fruit fly, black army cut worm, flea beetle, leaf roller, and thrips, and such diseases as twig blight, leaf spot, red leaf, and witches broom. Progress has also been made in the development of weed killers to destroy lambkill, sweet fern, hardhack, gray birch, and other weed plants.

A portion of the blueberry industry tax is used to forward extension work. County agents in the blueberry belt have been active; and since 1950, Ralph C. Wentworth, who was for thirty years county agent in Knox and Lincoln Counties, has been part-time blueberry specialist. The duty of Extension has been to take the finding of research out into the field and set them at work. Methods employed have included meetings, news articles, calendars of work, circulars and bulletins, and personal contact. County agents have kept careful watch for the first appearance of insects and diseases. They learn when the fruit fly begins to emerge at Blueberry Hill Farm and notify growers that the time has come to dust. They are ever on the alert for new developments.

How much has the blueberry industry grown since it burst the bounds of Washington County and became statewide? The following figures published by the Maine Agricultural Experiment station in its popular bulletin, "Producing Blueberries in Maine," will answer that question.

Annual Volume, Price, and Amount Paid for Blueberries By Maine Processors

Years	Average volume purchased annually in 100 lbs.	Average price per lb.	Average value paid annually
1924-27	6,978	7.86 ¢	$ 548,338
1928-32	8,741	5.23	457,389
1933-37	8,247	5.23	431,457
1938-42	11,257	5.95	669,407
1943-47	10,685	14.98	1,600,979
1948-52	18,587	11.92	2,215,141
1953-54	20,407	12.48	2,545,879

Part of the volume purchased by Maine processors came from Canada. In recent years these purchases have amounted to between two and three million pounds annually.

Maine blueberries are marketed in three different forms; fresh, canned, and frozen. In recent years only about one percent of the crop has been sold fresh, around thirty percent has been frozen, and the remainder has been canned.

The more important blueberry counties are along the Maine coast and in southwestern Maine," wrote Director George F. Dow, of the Maine Agricultural Experiment Station, in the bulletin just mentioned. "According to the 1949 Census, Washington County produces one half of the total crop, amounting to 4.4 million quarts in 1949. The combined crop in Knox and Lincoln Counties was 2.1 million quarts. Hancock is reported as having 1.7 million quarts, and Waldo was next with 0.4 million. All other counties combined comprised a total of only about 0.2 million quarts.

The most serious competition to Maine's native wild blueberries is the production in New Jersey and Michigan, which consists primarily of cultivated berries that are large sized and hand picked. The census reports a 1949 crop of four and a half million quarts in New Jersey and slightly over one million in Michigan. The comparable production in Maine was 8.8 million quarts.

The present outlook is for increased production both in Maine and elsewhere. That means keener competition, which in turn calls for more efficient production, processing, and marketing. On the other hand, the various components of the Maine industry are now more accustomed to working together toward common goals, and are better equipped to attain any goals that may challenge them than ever before.

14

THE MAINE EXTENSION SERVICE

Dennis Abdulla was appointed the first Blueberry Specialist of the Maine Extension Service in 1962. However, considerable attention had involved blueberry research, and resulting assistance to producers, from the time of the blueberry maggot disaster in 1924, the black army cutworm in 1944, and establishment of the Blueberry Hill research farm in 1946. Moody Treavet of the Extension Service published several bulletins from his research on nutrition and growth of blueberries, including #581 in 1959 and #605 in 1962. It appeared that a new disease problem occurred about every year. It is probably more accurate to state, as Herb Hanscom suggested, that most if not all of these problems already existed in blueberry fields; that they were just not identified until the Extension researchers were called in to explain a patch of bushes that showed damage. Amr A. Ismail followed Abdulla as Extension Blueberry Specialist, then Tom DeGomez, followed by David Yarborough who has filled the position since 1991.

This is a far from complete attempt to accurately determine the responsibilities of the Extension Blueberry Specialist. From the records of their activities, I believe that any job description would end with *and more*. I add here only copies of the headings of their regular publications, "Wild Blueberry Fact Sheet," and *The Wild blueberry Newsletter*, (previously *Blueberry News*), as samples from which some of their work is reported to the industry, and to add between following chapters, selected excerpts of time-relevant past publications.

Blueberry Information Guide

COOPERATIVE EXTENSION SERVICE
UNIVERSITY OF MAINE
ORONO

DISEASES OF LOWBUSH BLUEBERRIES

COOPERATIVE EXTENSION SERVICE
University of Maine

University of Maine, and the
U. S. Department of Agriculture
Cooperating

Orono, Maine
Dec. 3, 1962
Deering Hall

BLUEBERRY TEXTBOOK

IV. LOWBUSH BLUEBERRY FERTILIZATION

COOPERATIVE EXTENSION SERVICE

UNIVERSITY OF MAINE AT ORONO, MAINE 0446°

BLUEBERRY

NEWS

Newsletter No 3.　　November 19, 1984

Wild Blueberry
NEWSLETTER

UNIVERSITY OF
MAINE
Cooperative Extension

Toll-free Number 1-800-897-0757(US and Canada)

July 1997

Wild Blueberry
FACT SHEET

THE UNIVERSITY OF
MAINE
COOPERATIVE EXTENSION

The changing appearance of blueberry information sheets from the
Maine Extension Service.

15

THE WINNOWER

From the beginning of the canning of blueberries, the factories winnowed the berries, a process of cleaning them of dust, dirt, leaves, sticks, and other foreign material, before cooking. At first, they adapted the shaker process, which they already used to clean dry beans before cooking. This consisted of passing them over shaking screens of a size that the berries would fall through. An additional fan arrangement may have been added to blow off the lighter material.

The growers in the meantime, in an effort to deliver a better quality product, began removing the grass from the filled rake by hand and winnowing during the raking process. The first method, undoubtedly, was simply to hold them high above the basket in which they emptied their rakes, and let any wind that might be blowing separate much of the trash before the berries reached the basket. Some early machines may have produced wind from hand operated fans, and during the 1930s, a machine with the hand operated fan plus some method of passing the berries through the artificial wind to clear them of debris was being used by some growers.

By 1947, Emil Rivers of Rockland, Maine, a machinist, was advertising his blueberry cleaner and rakes. With slight modifications, the Rivers winnower was the only mechanical winnower used in the blueberry fields over a period of about fifty years. It eventually lost favor because of its size and weight, requiring two people to move it about the field, and smaller lighter shaker-

type machines took their place. More recently, with less refuse because of alternate year burning, and cleaner fields due to herbicides, hand raked berries go to the processor without being field winnowed, and mechanical rakers winnow on the machine.

(above) Motor driven winnower on a pickup.

(opposite) Contemporary motor driven shaker [winnower].

Early hand-powered winnower at Blueberry Hill Farm. Photo by
Natalie Peterson.

Emil River's large field blueberry cleaner had a capacity of 500-1,000 pounds per hour. The company is no longer in business.

PART III: WESLEY

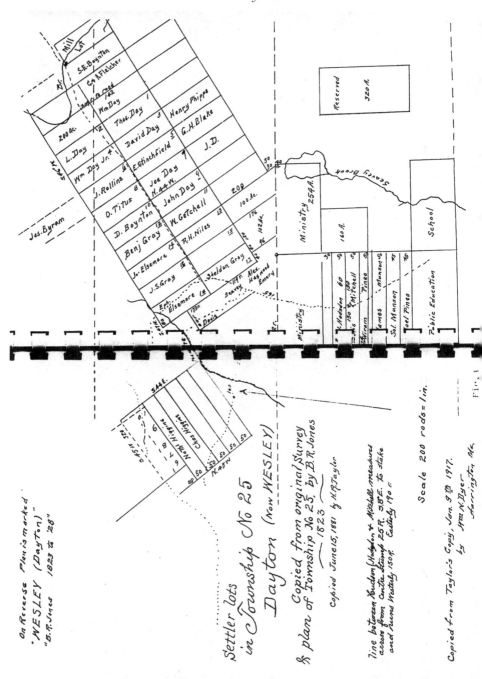

Early map of Wesley, originally called Dayton. Courtesy Wesley
Historical Society.

16

GREAT MEADOWS RIDGE

Before Wesley was renamed to honor the minister of that name who established the Methodist church, the town was known as Great Meadows Ridge. The original name came from the numerous meadows along the East (Machias) River. The meadows, in turn, were the result of numerous dams along the river that had been built by the loggers to store water on which to float their logs down the river. When the logging finished and the dams had washed out, the pond areas came naturally into meadow hay.

From *The History of Wesley, Maine*:

> To start a farm in the wilderness took men and women of courage and strong determination. First they cleared some land and built a crude dwelling with logs. Once they had cleared an acre or two they put in a crop. Sometimes they planted between the stumps, a most difficult task. The first year, the brush and worthless logs were burned and the ashes spread over the ground before planting. As soon as they could they would build a good barn. It was more important to have a good barn for the hay and cattle than to have a good house.

They also depended on deer in the forest and fish in the streams as part of their livelihood. They made their own corned beef and salt pork, sheared their own sheep, made sugar from the maples in the spring, cut ice from the nearby ponds, packing it in sawdust for the summer, and in the fall they cut many cords of wood for their fire-places and new fangled iron stoves. The sheep ran loose and each farmer put his own special mark on his sheep's ear.

William Day with his wife and family were among the first set-tlers in Wesley. He moved east from the coastal town of Phippsburg, followed a spotted trail up the East Machias River to the recently surveyed road from Bangor to Calais, and settled by a bubbling spring near the eastern end of the ridge. Other members of the Day family, including William P. Day from Leeds, Maine, were early settlers nearby. Each of the William Days had thirteen children. The area, becoming known as The Pines by about 1890, consisted of nine families, and Lincoln Day's daughter, Lulu Day Brigham wrote of the lives of that small community in which she grew up. The original paper has survived and is recorded in *The History of Wesley, Maine*.

During the same period, or within a generation, when the Bangor-Calais road had acquired stagecoach service, members of the Day family settled at the westerly end of the ridge, near the outlet to Chain Lakes.

It was not until about 1900 that Wesley became a blueberry town. The pioneer settlers cleared the land, moved the rocks, and developed the big fields to produce hay to feed the oxen and hors-es used to harvest the virgin forest. Slowly, when there became no need for the hay, blueberries spread into the fields, providing a marketable product for the landowners.

The Days and The Guptills, though dominating the town dur-ing certain periods, were by no means the only pioneer families of Great Meadows Ridge and Wesley, to which many of the current generations can trace their lineage. Among the names of those early families were Hayward, Durling, Carlow, Seavey, Love, Torrey, Gray, Driscol, Blake, Hawkins, and Rollins. Certainly there are others.

17

WESLEY

The identification on a map of Wesley, dated 1824, naming landowners at that time, includes *formerly Dayton*. Though some of the original settlers by the name of Day living in the Pines area had apparently sold their property by this date, it seems possible that the area may have previously been referred to as *Daytown* because nearly all of the residents had originally been of the Day family.

The General Cobb Road, from Bangor to Calais, through Township 25 was surveyed as early as 1763, but was hardly more than marked until some work was done on it during the war of 1812. General Cobb became land agent for the Bingham-Baring grants in 1820. Wanting to induce settlement along the route, he used his influence to improve the road, but it was not until 1857 that the road was considered adequate for a stagecoach, which carried mail and encouraged travel. Even then, landowners and merchants on the alternate road along the coast vigorously dissented. They advertised in local papers that the bears and wolves made travel through the wilderness unsafe. The route started out with sixteen horses, exchanging pairs at eight stops en-route and making the ninety-five miles in one day.

Larger stagecoaches later replaced the original ones, and teams of four, and when conditions demanded—such as times of mud and deep snow—teams of six, sometimes eight, horses were used. Settlement had extended off the ridge along the surveyed line toward Bangor. Stagecoach stops were established at the inns

View from Day Hill, Wesley.

along the way, about twenty miles apart, to change horses and to provide food and rest for those riding. The townspeople welcomed the opening of a shorter route to Bangor and the travel through their community. In later years it became known as The Airline Road.

The town was settled by hardy pioneers from along the coastal and westerly sections of the state. The road to the coast, from Wesley to Machias, was opened in 1835. The area was heavily wooded, and logs for home and barn building were sawed at local mills. Others were floated down the East and West Machias Rivers to larger mills on the coast or shipped on coastal sailboats to Bangor or Boston markets.

The pioneers cleared the land, burned the stumps, planted their gardens, developed the large hay fields to feed the horses, oxen, and cattle necessary for their logging efforts. A large measure of their food was gathered from an abundant supply of deer, ruffed grouse, snowshoe rabbits, and other wildlife.

The importance of the wildlife in the area is emphasized by quotes recorded in *The History of Wesley, Maine*, including the following:

1882 was called a disastrous hunting season. The number of deer shipped from Maine exceeded 2000, and not one in ten of the saddles shipped before the ponds froze had a bullet hole upon them. Of those with heads on, nine out of ten were shot in the back of the head, proving they were slaughtered in the water, driven into ponds by hounds. There were lots of 'Market Hunters' in those days. During those years they had 'Shakers', young fellows who liked to hunt, and who spent a lot of time in the back woods camps. They paid little attention to the laws. Some of the Wesley Shakers were J. Wilbur Day (whose autobiography has been published), Leverett Elsmore, Devereau Fenlason, and Eben Coffron.

Wilbur Day's escapades, including tangles with the law and jail time, are legend. It was not until 1919 that Maine residents were required to purchase a hunting license, but poaching occurred much earlier when season and deer limits prevented hunting at any time to fill the family meat needs. Such restrictions on living off the land were sharply resented by the local population and wardens were slow to enforce the laws. The license cost twenty-five cents, and it was good for life. My father had one. The state did renege and required annual licenses some time later.

Undoubtedly, unaware of its future, the town of Wesley spent many years preparing to become a blueberry town. First, oxen and horses were no longer needed for the cutting of timber, leaving no use for the hay they had grown on large fields that extended down from the homes along the ridge to the almost endless forest beyond. Wesley and much of Washington County experienced a period of poverty and reduced population following the Civil War, as there was decreased demand for the cutting and marketing of their virgin timber. There was an exodus of young men to the gold fields of Colorado, California, and Alaska. The girls left for the cotton mills of the larger cities. Some of the men went to Canada for the seasonal grain harvest, and when they returned to maintain the family farms, with the money they had saved, they bought up adjoining land that had been abandoned.

To utilize the hay fields, they raised more sheep, and because sheep much preferred grass and other brush growth to blueberry bushes, the blueberry fields experienced increased growth. As a result, at the time when blueberries were experiencing increasing demand, the town of Wesley had the product.

About 1900, Wentworth Leighton moved up from Columbia, near the barrens area, and purchased the Stinchfield farm on Day Hill. It had previously been owned by Henry Day. Leighton would have been aware of, and may well have raised, or at least raked, blueberries in Columbia. The Henry Day farm appears not to have been an active farm, that is, the fields not pastured or plowed for long enough that blueberries had spread over sufficient area for Mr. Leighton to produce a marketable crop.

Other farms in the Wesley area were soon producing blueberries. Frank Gray was reported to have delivered fifty bushels of blueberries on his horse hauled buckboard from Wesley to Cherryfield. It was a three-day roundtrip journey. A canning factory was operating in Machias as early as 1881, only twenty miles from Wesley. One would assume that most of the local berries would have been marketed there, unless other markets offered a considerably better price, or a factory agent from Cherryfield arranged for their purchase.

By, or shortly before 1900, most, if not all, of the open areas in the town were growing blueberries. Growing wild blueberries in the town of Wesley was in its infancy when Alexander Guptill moved to what is now named Guptill Road in Wesley, about 1917. Several of his sons were full-grown and on their own. Thatcher, with a younger brother, promptly left to spend five years in the logging camps of Minnesota. Perley remained in Machias for a few years before migrating to New York.

18

DAY HILL

The blueberry growers of Wesley, and of the nearby towns of Crawford, Alexander, Northfield, and Cutler—in fact, the entire eastern portion of Washington County, were relative latecomers to growing blueberries for the commercial market. Limited by the lack of a nearby canning factory (the first being in Machias about 1881), and with the railroad not arriving until 1898, and gasoline vehicles not generally available until about 1915, the commercial market was restricted to horse and wagon transportation and that was further limited by how long the berries would remain edible. Though some fresh blueberries were undoubtedly carried to markets on the stagecoach, perhaps even delivered to factories, the volume was small.

The deserted hay fields and pastures came naturally into blueberries around the turn of the century, just as the canning factories were increasing their demand. For the most part, those owners who had inherited the family farms were monarchs of their castles as it were, living off the land, or what might be better described as harvesting nature's bounties. However, once they began growing blueberries for market, they were vulnerable to the same difficulties that confronted all those dependent on agriculture to make a living. Not the least of these were personal health, weather conditions, and availability of labor as it was needed. Other variables included year-to-year fluctuations in crop size and quality, and subsequent market conditions. A good growing season didn't necessarily mean a good year, as regional increases in production could cause market prices to drop.

Old and new towers on Day Hill.

As a result, the farmers' perspective and the methods they employed to survive were considerably different from those who purchased and marketed their product. While those processing the berries eventually came to feel the effects of the grower's problems, it was always the grower who first experienced, recognized, and made efforts to solve the problem.

The blueberry rake, with its tines, pan, and reverse handle, had been invented and was in common use before farms on Day Hill and the immediate area were raising blueberries commercially. They were undoubtedly picking, even raking them where they grew wild in the pastures that were used for grazing the horses, oxen, sheep, and the family cow. They may have dried them, and certainly put them up in glass jars for winter use. As the berry market increased, with the potential for a rare cash market, they paid more attention to protecting the growth and expansion of the low-bush berry. They cut back the competing growth, pulling the taller weeds and young trees by hand, mowing where blueberry bushes were growing in the old hay fields. Their large families, local relatives, and neighbors without blueberry fields of their own became captive pickers and rakers who benefited as the cash received for berries began to trickle down.

Their primary market was the canning factory. Few, if any, early-ripened berries were sold. The early-ripening berries could not be raked, because of so many green berries, but they could be hand picked, which though fine for filling the family larder, was too slow a process for commercial use.

In the early days, the fields had been burned every two or three years, or until competing weeds reduced the crop, and old growth blueberry bushes interfered with raking. Meadow hay was cut and the hay spread on the blueberry fields after harvesting to promote more effective burns. Twice each year, families and neighbors gathered to provide support during the labor-intensive periods of burning and raking.

To control a burn, barrels of water were transported on horse-drawn hay wagons. Participants carrying buckets and brooms would visit, while waiting patiently for the morning dew of spring to dry. The field was ready to spring into flame when the bent end pipe torch was dragged along the down-wind side of the field. The torch was a simple homemade tool, half-inch pipe, bent at one end, in which a wick of rags extended for a few inches. The barrel of the pipe was filled with kerosene; the wick lit. A single match was sufficient to ignite a line of fire the length or breadth of the biggest blueberry field. Backfires, if required, could swiftly be ignited, and the crew with their buckets and brooms kept the fire under control, limiting it to the desired burning area. It was an annual party of friends and neighbors of all ages.

The three harvest weeks in August could have been considered pre-school days, in that children of all ages were a majority of rankers. Pre-school is an adequate description, because all members of the family attended, from breast-fed babies to baby-sitting great grandparents. More than harvesting the berries, it was the annual neighborhood visiting period, on the field, and from field to field. Bright colored jackets and shirts spotted the fields, as young and old bent to scoop the berries into buckets, and fill the bushel boxes to ready the berries for transport to the processing plants.

Fields varied. The original home field, which once grew hay, was level and free of rocks and clumps of bushes. The rocks that had been removed formed walls, separating the front yard from the road that passed in front of the house, and separating an adjoining pasture from which no rocks had been removed. The slowly rotting stumps of giant pines are still visible among a patch of white maple and willow brush. But the berry bushes seemed more vigorous, greener, and lush when closer to the stumps or rocks. Some owners had purchased the adjoining land of an abandoned farm. Often the buildings of the acquired farms had been burned or left to rot. The stone walls remained to map out the old home field and pastures. Quarried granite guarded the cellar hole; lilacs bloomed where they might have been seen from a kitchen window, and near the road, a rose bush that once greeted visitors. Rough rocky terrain marked which of the cleared areas had been fields and which had been pastures.

Common to every open space were the wild lowbush blueberry bushes. They surrounded the one-room schoolhouse and encroached the boundaries of the cemetery and grew in the yard in front of the horse stables beside the Grange Hall and church.

Blueberries remained wild, but attempts were being made to tame them.

19

WESLEY FAMILIES ABOUT 1930

It was a period in time when the residents of Wesley would make their decisions to remain in the town and participate in growing blueberries, or to leave for greener pastures. Among those who stayed and developed their blueberry fields were Thatcher Guptill, Harold Day, Harry Hayward, Went Leighton, Roger Gray, John Roberts, and Charles Sprague. In about 1917, Perley Guptill, though living in Machias, and Harold Day, living in Wesley, purchased a sizeable blueberry field situated across the Airline Road from the two-room schoolhouse on Day Hill. After a few years, Perley purchased Harold's half and took an active interest in the blueberry industry. He moved to Essex, near Albany, in New York State. In the early 20s, he hired Carl Day (later Dean Guptill) to tend the fields, although he would return with his family for two weeks each August to harvest the blueberry crop. The blueberries were sold to the Gaddis Canning Company in East Machias.

Perley accepted a position of managing a farm on the Whitney estate, just outside of Albany, in about 1928. His son, Charles, started a business in nearby Cohoes, New York in 1931. Meanwhile, the family continued to make a vacation of picking blueberries in Wesley two weeks every August. They tented on the land and kept an evening bonfire where neighboring natives would join them for impromptu parties. Thus, sons Charles Jr. and William (Billy) grew up with the blueberry business.

Of the current residents of Wesley that can trace their lineage to the original settlers who migrated to Great Meadows between

1820 and 1840, William Hayward and his wife Nellie (Guptill) both
were born and grew up on Day Hill. They were children to owners of substantial acreage of blueberry fields, and attended the
same (still existing) two-room grade school. As family members,
they participated in the labors involved in producing and marketing the wild lowbush blueberries, burning, weeding, and harvesting. Nellie, who was born in 1925, recalled that her first small blueberry rake had a straight back handle and short tines, more a learning rake with which five year-olds might participate. Not many
years after she first picked up that rake, she saved every penny
received during the harvest and purchased her first bicycle. She
was paid 25 cents per bushel on a one-year burn, and 35 cents on
a two-year burn. It was during the depression years, when the canning factories paid as low as 5 cents per pound. Only by hard work
and persistence were Nellie's wishes translated into a bicycle.

Her father, Thatcher Guptill, kept a cow and some beef cattle
and a pair of horses. The cattle were pastured during the summer,
along with those of his neighbors, on a meadow far up the main
Machias River. They visited the cattle frequently to offer grain and
salt to keep them tame until it was time to herd them back home
in the fall. Nellie, her sister, and three brothers were but part of the
crew of rakers that harvested Thatcher's fields, then went on to
neighboring fields, until all of the area berries were harvested.
Thatcher also furnished transportation, in an ancient truck, to take
their berries to market, thirty miles away, in Cherryfield. The
berries were loaded at the end of each harvest day, and an older
brother, Shirley, usually drove the truck. He took Nellie along to
keep him awake, and it was not unusual that she, though under-
age and without a license, often drove the truck home, late at
night, over the long lonely road from Cherryfield to Wesley, while
Shirley got some much-needed sleep.

Nellie's mother, Hattie (Durling), after marriage to Thatcher
had inherited a blueberry field on the other side of Route 192 from
one of Thatcher's fields. Berries from Hattie's field had tradition-
ally been sold to Stewart, Thatcher's sold to Wyman, competing
canneries in Cherryfield, and they saw no need to change either

arrangement. That was despite the fact that at each of the canneries they would have to wait in line with others delivering berries, while tests were made for fly maggots. Their trips were further extended, as not wanting to load empty boxes at the end of the first stop, which would have blocked unloading of berries at the second stop, made it necessary to make a return trip to the first factory for empties, and always there was a waiting line.

At that time, berries were shipped in half-bushel boxes, 16 x 15 x 5 1/2 inches. They were filled from the smaller end, over which a cover was nailed to prevent spilling. The boxes belonged to the canning company, with the company name impressed and painted on each box. It was the grower's responsibility to return all of the boxes. The sampling of the berries for fly maggots required prying the cover off from the sample box and nailing it back on, adding to the delays. If a grower, still raking at the end of day, had filled all of the empties brought back the night before, he might borrow boxes from a neighbor, resulting in the mixing of several source boxes. At one time, it was reported that Wyman, being short of boxes, went to a competitor's factory and claimed all of the full boxes with the Wyman imprint. It's changed some now. Today's boxes, which are made of plastic, and identified by color, are filled flat. At the end of each season, owners return the boxes to their original processors.

Nellie remembers the tents on a field next to her father's, where rakers from Machias, Marshfield, and Calais stayed while raking W. Leighton's big field where the fire tower still stands. They would cook their meals over campfires. Sprague, with large fields between Wesley and Machias, built a hotel that housed the Micmac Indians and others, during the August raking season.

Although considerable grass grew in the blueberry fields, hay was added to ensure a complete burn and satisfactory pruning. Marsh hay was plentiful among the dead-water lengths of the East River, Beaver Dam Stream, Old Stream, and other areas. The marsh hay that would not grow on the drier rocky soil on the ridge was preferred over the field, English hay, because it didn't seed hay in the blueberry fields. The tall meadow hay, growing in bunches in the wet and slimy soil, was cut with hand scythes, hauled on horse-pulled hay wagons after the berry harvest during the usual seasonal dry period, then spread on the blueberry fields. Again, as with harvesting the berries, cutting, hauling, and spreading the meadow hay was a family chore.

Carl Day, after military service, and several years of handling horses at a wealthy estate in New Jersey, returned to Wesley with his city born bride, Eleanor. Always a lover of horses, Carl purchased a pair. He worked them during the winter months, logging on the paper company lands, and then did local jobs during the summer. The first summer, he took a job cutting and hauling meadow hay for a local blueberry grower. He loaded his wagon with a tent and supplies for a week, and with Eleanor, drove down the hill along the bush-grown road, to the edge of a heath of tall meadow grass by Beaver Dam Stream. They set up the tent on a level area close to where the road broke out of the alders and tethered the horses in a broken down hovel that had long before been left by loggers.

In the morning, before leaving with his scythe to cut the meadow grass, Carl loaded his double-barrel shotgun, leaned it against a tree, and told Eleanor that if a bear should come around, the horses would smell the bear, become uneasy, and squeal, and that she should shoot the bear. Hearing the shot and not being far away, he would then come in a hurry and quiet the horses so they would not run away.

Eleanor sat close to the shotgun, ready to grab it at the least sound, and soon heard something crashing down the road through which they had come the night before. She grabbed the gun—was waving rather than aiming it—as she shivered in fear, when a horse and wagon, with a man driving it, came through the alder brush at the road entrance. Seeing her, the man began waving his arms and shouting, "Don't shoot, don't shoot. Put the gun down, put the gun down!"

20

THE GUPTILLS

Perley Guptill died in 1960. His son Charles had started with a gasoline filling station in Cohoes, New York, and steadily expanded it, selling International Harvester tractors, developed a construction business, and was involved in state land and power reclamation. His interest in, and love of the state of Maine and the blueberries continued, and he looked forward each year to the two-week blueberry picking vacation.

When returning from Maine in 1960, he packed fresh berries in dry ice and took them back to New York. They were sorted on the kitchen table, and marketed to local bakeries. The following year, he rented a refrigerated truck, rented freezer space near his home, and took a small truckload of berries back to New York. Now, with frozen berries the family could sort, pack, and sell as customers needed them over a period of time. They took pains to market a quality product, and the demand increased. In 1966 they built a small freezer plant in their barn in order to have storage space to accommodate their customers for the whole year. Demand increased, and they bought more blueberry land in Wesley when landowners moved away or became too old to care for their land. In 1969, the Guptills purchased two refrigerated Fruehauf trailer trucks. The berries were packed into the trucks directly from the fields, taken to New York, where they were processed, packaged, and marketed. By 1974, they needed more freezer space and built a larger, more efficient building in New York. They continued to invent new and improved equipment for processing the berries and their berries were in demand over a wider market area.

The thick summer fogs of Downeast Maine are perfect for raising blueberries. Photo by Natalie Peterson.

Charles died in 1974, leaving the blueberry business to his wife Peggy and his sons Charles Jr. (Skip), and William (Billy). Two years later, they built a freezer plant in Wesley, and moved their processing equipment to the Maine land that their grandfather had purchased fifty years earlier. The berries were still shipped to New York for storage and distribution. They steadily improved land-use practices, experimenting with fertilizers to improve the harvest and berry quality. Hardly a year passed that new and improved processing methods and equipment were not made. They purchased more blueberry land and purchased berries from local producers.

Guptill Farms provided seasonal employment to many area individuals of all ages to grow the crops, mow, burn, and rake; and in the plant to handle the incoming berries, sorting and packing for shipment, and trucking them to New York. For many years, Eleanor Day supervised the crew of eight women who, sitting on each side the moving belt, would remove the green berries and any other material that had passed through the winnowing and washing processes, then would weigh and pack them in thirty pound boxes for shipment.

Guptill's processing plant, Wesley. Photo by Natalie Peterson.

Source and owner and weight of berries were recorded as they were unloaded from trucks bringing them from the fields. The empty boxes, repaired if necessary, were loaded back onto the trucks to be filled again. The big blue attractive refrigerated trailers, now painted with GUPTILL FARMS, MAINE WILD LOWBUSH BLUEBERRIES were loaded, with Buddy Day, or other drivers, guiding them over the long trip to Cohoes, N.Y.

For the most part, Billy was the engineer and inventor of the processing division. Skip handled the field requirements, from mowing and raking to burning, and kept a steady supply of berries arriving at the plant during the harvest season. The Guptills continued to live in New York, and operated the processing plant for only two weeks each August.

In both marketing and in processing, the Guptill operation was completely independent of other Maine processors, except that the field price paid the growers always was the same. For one reason

Fresh from the field blueberry fields being hoisted to begin processing. Photo by Natalie Peterson.

or another, not all of the local growers sold their berries to
Guptill's. Some had previously joined a cooperative, others continued to market to Maine processors to whom their parents had
sold for years. However, the Guptill plant was always available to
anyone with berries to sell.

Asked what the incentives were that promoted or dictated the
annual improvements and growth of the processing facilities, Billy
stated; "I think through those years everybody was looking for a
better and cleaner berry to take to market, and it really started for
us, probably in the early '60s. My father developed several
machines there in New York to break up the berries. They arrived
(in New York) frozen in (half-bushel) wooden boxes. The berries
were in wooden boxes just as they had come from the field. They
arrived partially frozen in the freezer trailers and were kept another two weeks in our freezer in New York before they could be further processed. We had to break up the clusters, loosen them, in
order to sort (clean) them; blow leaves and anything out; then they
had to be hand picked (over). It was a very slow process because
you had to virtually pick up a berry and take the stem off to be
sure it was clean.

Bill Guptill. Photo by Natalie Peterson.

Guptill Farm trucks.

"The berries that were ripe would always have the stem off, but the ones that were not quite ripe enough would always have the stem on and one had to break it off. So there was a lot of manual labor at first, and it was not until about 1976 when we could actually freeze the berries here (in Wesley) and bring them down to a temperature in a unit we called a squirrel cage. It would really do the de-stemming process for us and actually break the berries off. That's because they were frozen and the stems were brittle.

"The improvements to the line are almost continuous over every single year. Because every year was (different)…you might have a year there was a drought, you might have a year there was too much rain, and the berries would be too soft. You might have had a bad judgment call on picking a little too late, or couldn't get help and pick too late which made the berries soft. So each year you developed new pieces of equipment to put into the line to actually try to improve over the problem you had the previous year."

Since moving the processing activities and freezing facilities from New York to Wesley, and without local freezer storage, the berries were still shipped to New York, the two big trailers making daily trips. This continued until freezer storage was built in Wesley in 1992.

Asked about competition, and if they exchanged information, Billy in conversation with me said, "There was very little exchange (with other processors). I did not know the other processors in the early years. I think throughout that time period we felt that we could create a better berry, a cleaner berry than what we were seeing from others, and we felt that it was our niche in the market to have a very high quality, frozen berry."

When asked if competitors were also freezing berries when they started freezing, Billy answered, "Not locally. I would say that probably in Ellsworth, Wyman, and Stewart were doing some form of frozen product, but I don't know the exact processes they were going through at that time. Oh yes, we were very much in the beginning of freezing, and everyone had a little different idea— after all, they're all Mainers—on how to do it. So each person was going down his own path."

Billy admitted that they made errors and false starts in developing their processing system, and today it continues to be improved.

Blueberry field in Stockton Springs, Maine.

PART IV: PERSONAL EXPERIENCE

The author's son Jim with rake and berries.

21

MY FIRST COMMERCIAL HARVEST

What I had learned from reading and questioning those who raised blueberries nearby, before Shirley Guptill told me he would no longer harvest or manage the blueberry field, was of more interest than actual education to combat the problems I would encounter in the days and years ahead. Nothing could replace what was learned from personal experience on the job.

The morning after Shirley had told me of his decision to release the blueberry field to me, I drove to the lot, two miles south from Route 9 on the road to Machias. I parked in the end of the woods road that extended east through the blueberry field and into the woodland beyond. Standing in the road, I looked over the expanse of property that for the first time seemed to be mine. My new familiarity prompted recognition of that spot as the one where Chet and I had dragged out our deer along the crusted snow-covered road thirty-five years before. I glanced southerly to the top of the low hill where Milt Roberts had spotted the big buck from outside his kitchen door, feeding in his nearby garden. The house was gone, but a caved-in cellar hole, and the nearby dug well remained. Blueberry bushes had overrun the garden area. It was my destiny, and I had returned.

Carl Day, the night before, had reminded me that I would need hay to spread on the area I would be harvesting, and he had already mowed and raked his big field, and would give me the hay. Son Jim had arrived a few days earlier to do some fishing, and he helped me haul several loads to the blueberry field, where we piled it near where it would be spread after the harvest. We were not surprised to see a fairly good crop of berries ready to be raked.

What would I do with the berries? Who would buy them? Where would I get the boxes used to ship them in? Would I need a winnower, and if so, where could I get one? I explained my predicament to Carl Day.

Carl assured me that the Guptill brothers, Skip and Billy, would buy the berries. Eleanor worked at the Guptill plant during two weeks of the harvest season. I was also assured that I could borrow a winnower, rakes if I needed them, and that I could buy string to mark the ricks, and anything else I needed, from the Guptill brothers.

I had, of course, seen the buildings, trucks, and boxes at the Guptill plant, which was located across from the schoolhouse and near the corner of the road to Machias and Route 9, the Airline Road. My blueberry field was only two miles from the plant. Carl and Eleanor had told me a lot about the Guptills. In addition to the plant, I was also aware that they seemed to own a lot of the big blueberry fields on both sides of the road over Day Hill.

When Jim and I were ready, we followed Carl to the Guptill plant where we met the Guptill brothers, borrowed a Rivers winnower, which they loaded on my pickup, with a supply of empty half-bushel wooden boxes, and a bale of cotton string suitable for marking out the ricks. Ricks are aisles between rows of string that identify the area for which a raker would be responsible.

Putting out the string, I was told by Carl, who had put out miles of it, deserved more attention than the simple statement led one to believe. The purpose being to mark the aisles that would guide the rakers, so as to be sure all the berries got raked. The cotton string was purchased in a round ball. With one end securely tied to a bush at the margin of the rick, it can be unwound as the individual putting it out walks in the direction that will mark the boundary of the rick. If it is a long distance, the string may be attached at desired spots to another bush, and again at the further end.

Returning parallel, the next string put out will determine the

Son Jim and Bill McKeage during the harvest.

width of the rick. It may be from four to eight feet in width, determined by the judgment of the individual putting it out, and considering factors such as how thick the berries are, how much weed
interference for the raker, are the rakers experienced or amateurs,
young or old, and perhaps the weather. All of these factors affect
the enthusiasm of the rakers, and may encourage, or discourage,
the speed and quality of the harvest.

On many fields it is not wise to put out any more string than is
necessary to start the crew the next morning, then setting the ricks
just ahead of them, so as not to leave a lot of ricks marked
overnight. A deer or a moose walking across or feeding in the field
during the night, dragging its feet, may stretch the string in various directions, and require that the lines be straightened before the
rakers get to such an area.

The string, of course, is a fragile barrier, and a raker, aware that
shifting the string to widen or narrow his rick may include a better patch of berries or avoid poor raking, is inclined, if unseen, to
take advantage of the situation. If the string is *bent* to avoid a spot
of poor raking, around a big rock or over a hole, and the raker
ahead of the raker in the next rick, that raker may straighten the

String being reeled in to be reused. Photo by Natalie Peterson.

string when he gets to it, to show that the raker ahead had not raked it.

On putting out the string, one must also take into consideration the length of the rick. The raker, with two buckets full of berries, must carry them to the winnower, and the distance, if uphill, or rough walking, increases his labor, and takes time from his raking. His pay is for berries winnowed, with no portal-to-portal allowance. While women and children may be assigned the narrower and shorter ricks, or a husband carry his wife's full buckets to the winnower, little preference can be shown without complaint.

Raking blueberries in a rick. Photo by Natalie Peterson.

Once the berries are raked, the string, if not removed, can become a problem as it collects on the mower cutter bar. There is also the consideration of its ten-dollar cost. It is impossible to rewind onto the small spool from which it was unwound. I tried a crumpled newspaper, coat hangers, and over my thumb and elbow, usually ending up throwing it away. A friend, apparently seeing one being used on a neighbor's field, made a reel eighteen inches in diameter and about four inches in width, with a hanging handle to carry it and a reel handle by which to turn it. With a small adjustment, it was convenient to reel in and to put out the string, and could be used to store the string for the next year. One could cut off the strings where attached at one side of the field, go to the other end of the ricks, and reel in the whole length, tie it to the end on the next rick, or across the field, and have an endless string for re-use.

On the shallow hillside of the southern section, next to the woods, I strung out the string. Jim and I started raking. Not long after we had started, when Jim a few yards ahead of me stood to clean his rake of grass, looked back and remarked, "We have company." And he pointed to back behind me. Only a few hundred feet away, a black bear was lunching in a lush patch of berries. I yelled to attract his attention. Bears do not see well but have keen hearing. He stood up, looked around, and slouched off to behind a small fir tree and out of sight. We saw him back again within fifteen minutes, but this time he paid no attention to us. Apparently satisfying his appetite, he left. We raked two bushels, four winnowed boxes, that day, quitting about noon because of very warm weather.

We continued the leisurely raking, increasing the quantity raked each day, but taking time out for some fishing, and not raking in the heat of the day. We were also overrun by relatives and friends whom we welcomed, and they picked a lot of berries. Guptill had mechanical problems in the processing plant and stopped accepting berries on August fifteenth. Seeing how many berries we still had left to be raked, Skip Guptill arranged for Herb Hanscom, buying for Medomac Canning Company, to take the berries. He also recommended that we hire Arnold Sours and son Clarence to help with the raking. They started raking on the eighteenth. Jim had left to go back to work, and old friend, Bill McKeage, replaced him. Bill, retired by then, had worked for me as a company employee. He had previous experience operating a winnower on a blueberry field in New Hampshire. He proved to be an expert at it, and had the ability to keep its cranky motor operating. He did all the winnowing, and helped, when time available, to rake berries.

Bill was dangerously allergic to bee stings. And on one of his forays to rake berries, and a hundred yards from his tube of protective pills left in the car, he was stung. Without a word, Bill dropped the rake and made a beeline for the pills. He arrived just in time.

We were averaging about forty boxes a day, with an estimated two days of very good picking ahead of us by August twenty-second, but arrived the next morning to find that during the previous

1990

MAINE BLUEBERRY TRANSPORT PERMIT

Date: _8/8/90_

1. Landowner where berries were harvested: _WALTER STAPLES_

   Address: _Box 252 WOODLAND ME_

   Phone Number: _454-7732_

2. Landowner where berries were harvested: _SAME_

   Address: _WESLEY_

   Phone Number: _____

3. Landowner where berries were harvested: _____

   Address: _____

   Phone Number: _____

Authorized Permit Holder: _WALTER STAPLES_

Drivers License #: _0955413131_

State or Province Issued: _NH_

Vehicle Description: _____

License Plate #: _389 /33_

State or Province Registered: _NH_

Signature of Permit Issuer : _Walter Staples_

Issuers Name (please print): _WALTER STAPLES_

MAINE BLUEBERRY COMMISSION

Edward J. McLaughlin, Executive Director
32 Coburn Hall, University Campus, Orono, ME 04469
(207) 581-1475

PERMIT   303

(Instructions on the back of Page 2 - Yellow copy) Page 2

Pulpwood harvested by the author.

afternoon or moonlit night, someone else had raked most of the remaining area. They came in over the stonewall from the south, on the back slope of the hill, where they could not have been seen from the road. The rustlers had taken advantage of a greenhorn, not unusual at the time.

It was a good crop, and the canning factory price was good. After taxes, and trucking expenses, net for the year amounted to $4,964.00, a third of the cost of the entire property a few years before. I suddenly became very enthusiastic about the blueberry business!

I located and purchased an old Cub tractor. I hauled it from New Hampshire to Wesley. I risked life and limb mowing around the huge rocks and over the holes in the old pastureland portion, but somehow survived the ordeal. I had previously hauled some hay from Carl Day's and piled it on the edge of the field. Now I hauled the rest of his hay and spread it rather thick over the newly mowed area.

After considering various ways that might help prevent rustling berries in the future, I moved the trailer from the central location to the top of the hill, one hundred feet from the road, by the well and cellar hole, near three old apple trees. The following August, I stretched a length of clothesline from the corner of the trailer to the nearest apple tree. I then hung a towel, a dishrag, and a couple of washcloths on the line, so that it appeared someone was staying there. I had no more trouble with the rustlers.

Before hunting season, besides cutting forty cords of spruce budworm devastated fir trees; I had hauled the rest of Carl's hay to the blueberry field and with what I had hauled before, spread it. About half the field, that part where we had raked berries, was ready to burn the next spring

Your Blueberry Tax Program

Most blueberry growers know that the blueberry tax was increased to 1 cent per pound by action of the legislature in 1984. It is important that growers understand how this money is collected and used. Following are brief explanations of some questions that growers may have.

How is the Blueberry Tax Collected?
The blueberry tax is shared equally with one half cent collected from growers and one half cent collected from processors or shippers. Tax returns and payments are submitted by the processors to the Maine Bureau of Taxation at the rate of 1 cent per pound. The usual practice is to deduct the growers share from payments made to growers for their blueberries.

How are Blueberry Tax Funds Used?
The primary purpose of the 1984 increase was to generate funds for promotion and expansion of the market for blueberries. At the same time, it was recognized that the blueberry industry maintain its support of blueberry research by the Maine Agricultural Experiment Station and for educational programs offered by the Extension Service.

Blueberry News, 11/19/1984

BLUEBERRY HARVEST

So many times today
I thought of Bill McKeage.
Though many harvest now
I've winnowed by myself;
I came here first with him.
He'd worked in berry fields,
Had run the winnower;
Not difficult, you say,
And I of course agree;
But berries cleaned by some
Were hardly cleaned at all.
They still had leaves and sticks,
Some caterpillars too.
As if by magic touch
When Bill had winnowed them,
The boxes capped with blue
Were ready for the cream
And waiting for a spoon.
The pride that Bill then had
That kept his berries best
His legacy to me
Through many harvests since.

22

STILL LEARNING

In the spring of 1979, before the effects of not having been burned the previous year were realized, I was told by my experienced neighbors, what to expect. At the end of March, I enticed sons Russ and Jim, and friend Bill McKeage to come to the camp for a weekend. I had brought bush cutters and scythes. I had pitchforks at camp. With our weapons of destruction, we descended on the south field and decapitated, or otherwise destroyed, much of the uncut weeds and bushes remaining in the field. We then spread the remaining hay that I had hauled from Carl Day's the previous fall. It was ready to burn when the hay and bushes had dried out and weather conditions permitted.

I was told of a federal program that would pay half of the cost of bulldozing a fire break road between blueberry land and adjoining forest land, and had signed up to participate. Jerry Torry, who lived in town and was employed by the forestry department, had a dozer and I hired him to do the work. Mud time on country roads had familiar memories for me, but frost out around the blueberry fields developed stickier problems. I got my pickup buried and Jerry stuck the dozer late one afternoon. We left the mud problems to be solved the next morning, and he gave me a ride back to camp.

I asked Jerry where he had come from and he told me Deblois, a town to the west between the Airline Road and Cherryfield. My grandfather with friends, many years before, made annual hunting trips to Deblois and a man named Torry was their guide. Could it have been his father? No, it was his grandfather. I

Burning the author's field.

recalled stories my grandfather had told me, some of which Jerry's grandfather had told him.

The next morning, April 20th, Jerry picked me up at camp. At the field, he was able to get the dozer out of the mud, then pulled my pickup back up to the highway. After work that night, I met Jerry at the forestry office, got a fire permit for the next day, and borrowed five Indian fire pumps. I had assurances from family that the manpower to burn the field would arrive at camp on time. The permit, which I signed, essentially stated that I accepted responsibility for any damage that a runaway fire might cause.

Sons, Russ, Jim, and Mark, with Bill McKeage, arrived late that night, and were ready to fight fire after a good breakfast. We loaded our equipment, including a couple of old brooms and a fire torch, which I had made, and a small can of kerosene. We filled the Indian fire pumps and our berry buckets with water from Rocky Brook where it crossed the road on our way to the field. Though it

The north end of the author's blueberry field.

was a fair day with bright sunshine, we considered the field too wet to burn, and after waiting for some time, went back to camp for lunch. Back to the field after lunch, and because of a northerly, light breeze, we started the fire on the southerly end of the south field next to a stonewall boundary with a neighboring field. We expected the fire burning into the wind would move more slowly, be easier to control. We had hardly started the fire over the width of the field and parallel to the wall, when, with a sudden gust, the wind changed to come now from the southeast, and the flames, well fed from the hay and bushes, went roaring out across the field. Leaving Bill to guard against another backlash, I, along with the rest of the crew, with Indian fire pumps strapped to our backs and extra buckets of water in the pickup, rushed to the midfield right-of-way, and started a backfire to prevent the fire from crossing the road and penetrating the forest. The importance of the firebreak road, just finished by Jerry Torry, was now evident, and

Burning blueberry fields in Aurora.

wide enough that the fire did not jump across. Action was fast and furious for a brief half hour, and the fire raced across the field so fast that it did not result in a good burn, but the fire was controlled, and no one was hurt.

The wind died down as quickly as it had started. Making sure that all hot spots were extinguished, we went back to camp for supper. Then we refilled our tanks and buckets with water, returned to the field, and burned the north field, fully under control at all times.

Back to the field the next morning, we checked for areas where the fire had skipped over the top, rather than burn deep, and were able to restart, and burn those areas more satisfactorily.

Neighbor Paul Seavey, who leased the field next to my south line, arrived with a crew to burn that field. He suggested that they could let the fire burn not only to the wall, but also across and to the edge of the burn in my field, Because of our problem the day before, and our fear that we could not stop the fire at the wall; we had left the bush area not burned. He, and his experienced crew, did a much better burning than we had done.

23

OLIVE AND CREW TO RAKE

I had spent considerable time at "Blueberryland" in early spring and during the summer. It had nothing to do with blueberries, except that while there I was able to observe the rapid spring growth of the bushes, the budding and bloom, and the bee activity, as well as discuss the current conditions with my neighboring growers. I was there to cut and yard pulp wood in an effort to salvage as much as possible from the effects of a spruce bud worm infestation that had killed my fir trees.

Because we had burned both the north and south portions of the field in the spring of 1979, I had none to burn in 1980. And, being there, seeing the Guptill brothers frequently, I knew before the blueberries were ready to harvest that they would not open their processing plant that year. They advised me to contact Gay Brothers in Marshfield, next to Machias, which I did. They had taken my berries before and were interested in getting them again.

On August 2nd my first visitors of the blueberry season arrived. Son Dan, his wife Trish, and their young son arrived and we spent the next several days fishing the nearby lakes. Before they left, we had picked four quarts of blueberries and, in a cutting near camp, as many, or more, wild raspberries. I strung out string to mark the ricks on August 5th. Gay's truck left a winnower and empty boxes. Mike Sullivan, who had rented the house across the road from the south end of my field, had been helping me with cutting pulp for some time. He and I started raking the area north of the dividing road on August 5th. We had a full house of berry

Rakers working in the field.

picking relatives, but were usually up, had breakfast, and left for the field before they stirred. Because of the morning fog that blanketed the area for a couple of hours each morning, it was always more comfortable raking early than in the heat of the day. Also, in the morning chill, the berries were more firm, less apt to crush. Jim and Bill McKeage arrived on the 8th to help with the raking.

The crop was average or better and my four-man crew was harvesting a reasonable amount of berries for the truck to pick up daily. I suppose, however, that Olive Getchel, raking on Gray's land, just over the wall from mine, with her crew of twenty or more, mostly children, and knowing more about raking blueberries than I would ever learn, was already aware that, with only four raking, it would take us until Thanksgiving to finish my fields. She may also have not had another field to rake when she finished at Gray's. Whatever the reason, Olive climbed over the wall, and came over to talk with me. Olive was a large, rugged woman, dressed in a rough shirt and skirt, her graying hair hanging loosely from a battered straw hat. She told me they would finish raking on Gray's in four or five days, and that if I needed rakers, she would bring her crew in to help finish my field.

I looked back over how much we had raked to date, and the

large area left to do, and realized I would need help. I told her I would probably need her help and that she should contact me when she was finished next door.

I asked neighbors about Olive. Her husband was our rural mail carrier. They lived in Marshfield. She was a real character. Her crew, of which she was very proud, was mostly school children. She was strict with them, but had a way with young children to which they responded. They were a noisy bunch that we could see and hear as we came closer to the wall that divided our fields, but it was the sound of happy children. I doubt they set any picking records, but they raked clean and harvested a satisfactory amount daily

On the 14th, during what was now her daily visit from over the wall, Olive told me that she had a young couple (not children) who had stayed in a small tent by the fallen down barn on the Gray field the night before and were raking for her that day. She did not really need them and would send them to help me if I wanted them. I did want them, and told her to tell them they could stay in my trailer. She said, "They're not married, but they are in love. They're good rakers, won't give you any trouble." Jim and Kim moved into my trailer and raked for me until we finished, though they asked for their pay, in cash, every afternoon, leaving me to wonder if they would be there the next morning.

We had moved to even better raking in the south field. Olive brought her crew over at ten-thirty on the 18th, and worked my field on the 19th. With Bill McKeage running the winnower, which saved the rakers the time spent while waiting in turn to winnow their own berries, we shipped fifty-five boxes on the 18th, and eighty-two boxes on the 19th. Olive borrowed my winnower to finish a field for Guptill, but was back the next two days. It was Friday night and we were almost finished. I went home for the weekend, came back Monday night and finished the raking, working alone, on the 27th.

Gay Brothers paid me $4,232.00 for the berries that we shipped to them. Clean-up included pick up, cleaning, and storage of equipment, the buckets, rakes, and the winnower, and removal of the accumulated refuse of paper cups, coke cans, water bottles, discarded clothing, several broken shipping boxes...the usual clutter following a harvest. I swept out the trailer, washed the floor and dishes, and had the bedding, towels and curtains washed before replacing them, and I padlocked the door before leaving.

It was mid or late September before I came back to camp for a fishing weekend. I stopped by to check the trailer. I removed the padlock and opened the door. I could not believe what I saw. The floor was littered with a dozen or more items of silky, obviously feminine underwear. At the far end of the room the bedding on the combination divan-bed was tangled and twisted, one pillow on the floor. Directly in front of me, and over the kitchen sink, the small push-out window had been removed.

Further investigation revealed that it had been the route of entrance and retreat. Screws holding the hinged window had been removed and the window, standing on end, was used as a ladder to reach the open space, and pull one's self through the small space onto the kitchen sink. Both entrance space and the underwear provided evidence as to size and agility of the visitors, probably teenagers. No permanent damage had been done. I replaced the window, padlocked the door, and went fishing to provide time to think of how to handle the situation. I certainly did not want to wage war with local teenagers, nor did I want to encourage continued use of the trailer for the obvious or any other reason. Later that afternoon, I returned to the trailer with a twenty-foot length of clothesline, and a package of clothespins. I fastened one end of the line to a corner of the trailer, the other end to an apple tree that left the line parallel to the road, some fifty feet away. I then, carefully, hung the underwear along the length of the line, where it swayed gently in the breeze, as if waving to passersby. I drove past the trailer early the next morning. My clothesline had been cut and what I had hung there the day before had been removed. It was too good a secret to keep, and I fully expect that some day I will hear the story repeated, not admittedly by one of the perpetrators, of course.

RAKING BLUEBERRIES

Three weeks I worked
In berry fields.
Three weeks I worked
From dawn 'till dusk.
A sandwich break
Perhaps at noon;
All other meals
Without daylight.
I cooked my food
Did dishes too.
I bent and raked
Then crawled and raked,
Filled buckets full.
The winnower
Then ate them up
And spewed them out
In boxes for
The factory.
So pale and weak
To start the job
I thought I'd die
By noon first day,
Was sunburned too,

Held rake so tight
A blistered hand
And worst of all
My aching back.
But now it's done.
The berries raked.
Hardly enough
Left for the birds.
My skin is brown.
My callused hands
No longer sore.
My muscles bulge.
My back is strong;
My wallet fat.

On looking back
I ask myself
If it were worth
The agony.
The answer is:
You bet it was.

24

NEGLECT AND RESULTS

With one year before retirement from my twenty-eight year employment with one company, the year was taken mostly with travel in the United States, Canada, and a ten-day trip to Italy in the middle of April. Both north and south portions of the field had been harvested in 1980, making it unnecessary to burn that spring, a result of having burned both in 1979. I made few spring trips to Wesley when black and burning fields and the warnings of friends reminded me that I would be raking a two year burn in August of 1981.

This seemed to be the opportune time to again divide the field into two parts, with a harvest each year; therefore, it was necessary to burn one part of it in 1981, thus reducing the 1981 harvest by half, as well as that half being a two year burn. Unable to get family and friends to help burn because of weather conditions, I asked Paul Seavey to burn the north portion, which he did on April 23rd.

I arrived at the camp the afternoon of August 4th, and the next morning visited Carl Day who went with me to Guptill Farms to borrow and help handle a winnower, and to load boxes I would need to get started. I started raking on the two-year burn of the south portion, by the woods road dividing the field. It was definitely more difficult, and slower, to rake the two-year bush growth, and the berries seemed to be mostly on the tips, rather than fruited low on the vines. There were fewer berries there, and they were much slower to rake if one was being careful not to crush them in the process. I was also delayed, and inconvenienced, not unwillingly, by a steady stream of visitors after berries

The author with Princess.

(providing frequent lobster dinners and other fancy meals), severe back pains (that required many aspirin), and temperatures always reaching 90 degrees before noon on fair days.

I averaged taking four winnowed boxes into Guptill's processing plant each day through August 10th, then Guptill closed for the season and again, Herb Hanscom picked up the rest of my berries for Medomac. The south end finished, I moved to the woodland side of the south field where the berries were a lot thicker and the raking much easier. Expecting son Jim to arrive the next day, I put out string to mark the ricks for a large area, and moved the winnower down past the little stream and across the road so that it would be nearer to where we would be raking.

I was raking the next morning before the fog had lifted, or the dew dried off the bushes. Suddenly, a small gray-brown bird swooped down and landed inches beyond the pointed teeth of my rake, stabbed a big green grasshopper that I had disturbed and proceeded to crush and swallow it. The bird, (he or she), hopped to and perched on a slightly higher bush, cocked its head as if listening, then looked directly up into my face, bent over to

Princess.

rake as I was, only about twenty-four inches away. It did not
chirp, or make any other noise or dip its tail or shrug its head,
until I moved my rake. Then, with its head down, it dived quickly into the bushes and came up with another grasshopper, this
one black and yellow, which it ingested with the same fervor as it
had the previous one.

Afraid that my movement would frighten the bird, I reluctant-
ly returned to normal action and speed to rake, and, for some time,
the bird continued to take advantage of my movements, which
would stir up the grasshoppers. At one time, taking advantage of
a full bucket of berries, it flew to the edge and dipped its head to
come up with, and eat, a particularly large and juicy berry, and
then another. The act may have lasted an hour before the bird
swooped from the edge of the bucket, circled my head, and flew
away. There were no color variations on its rather bland, gray-
brown feathers. It was smaller than a robin, larger than a sparrow.
It seemed to have a heavier beak, and I wondered if it might be an
immature grosbeak. Lacking any evidence of special effects or
brash actions, I considered it a female and I called her Princess.

Princess returned once, later in the day. Again she perched on a short bush just ahead of my rake and happily gorged herself on grasshoppers that I drove in her direction. There were other insects such as the big green tomato worm, slugs, bumblebees too fat to fly, butterflies, spiders, and salamanders. But Princess was either on a grasshopper diet or was hooked, at least temporarily, on grasshoppers with blueberry dessert.

Sons Jim, Russ, and my forever hunting and fishing partner, Big Russ, arrived the next afternoon…and we promptly went fishing. For the next week, Russ and Big Russ spent most of the time fishing, while Jim and I raked berries.

Princess returned each morning, and usually again later in the day. She frequently hopped to the edge of the bucket of berries and chose a few big juicy berries before returning to her grasshopper hunt. I held out my hand, thinking she might perch on a finger, but, though not afraid, she ignored the invitation. She occasionally left to feed on greener pastures ahead of Jim's rake, but ultimately showed no partiality between us.

Jim and I set a goal of a minimum of four boxes each per day, and averaged somewhat more than that. We did get in a reasonable amount of fishing, and we finished raking the berries and left for home on August 20th. Net income (and labor income since we did all the raking), amounted to $2,222, about half the crop on both north and south portions the previous year.

I had seen for myself the difference in raking and the quantity of berries between a one-year and a two-year burn. And I had personally experienced the added difficulty in raking the two-year bushes. I had established a marketing relationship with two processors. I was learning.

Fresh from the inconvenience of a borrowed winnower, I inquired if one might be purchased. Carl thought that a man only a mile up the road from my camp, then physically unable to rake his blueberry land, might have one stored in his barn. He did. It was a Rivers winnower, pretty well battered and patched, the belts missing. The owner was very pleased with my offer of seventy-five dollars, and I brought it home. A neighbor carpenter removed the patches and replaced the wooden parts. Applying a bit of paint, it looked as good as new. I was assured that Guptill Farms kept a supply of belts on hand and that I could get one from them the following year.

Blueberry Production Budget

Item	Quantity/acre	Unit price	Value/acre
Income: wholesale blueberries	1680	$.30	$504.00
Expenses			
a. Pruning			67.50
b. Weed control, applied	2 lbs.	25.00	50.00
c. Disease control, applied	24 ozs.	0.83	20.00
d. Pollination	1 hive	28.00	28.00
e. Insect control	1 pint	7.00	15.00
f. Harvest labor	1600 lbs.	0.15	252.00
g. Field and road maintenance	0.04 hrs.	40.00	1.60
h. Interest on operating capital, 5 months	106.50	12%	5.33
i. Management fee		7%	35.29
Fixed			
a. Property improvement			7.78
b. Property taxes	250.00	0.020	5.00
Total expenses			$487.50

Wild Blueberry Newsletter, November 1986

CHURCH SUPPER

Blueberry pie, Blueberry pies,
How many berries in a pie?
How many cooks, how many pies?
How many tongues and lips stained blue,
How many spots on shirts and pants
From pie that somehow slipped from forks?
No cooks alike but each her best;
If crust too short or pie too sweet,
It still will be the favorite
Of someone there who came for it.
The wild sweet taste from fields turned blue
Where sun and fog and bees have worked;
And children bent with iron rakes
And buckets full were winnowed clean
Of sticks and leaves they also raked.
Their tongues and lips perhaps are blue,
Not waiting for a pie be made.
Blueberry pie, Blueberry pies,
Please pass Aunt Maud's blueberry pie!

25

THE BLUEBERRY CYCLE

One has to find something more than the cash received, year after year, to look forward to raking the blueberries. It must overcome rising early; transportation through the fog (there is always thick morning fog in August in Maine); wading in the wet bushes; bending to push an awkward shaped rake under and up to scoop the berries; removing by hand the grass, leaves, and insects that stick to the rake; the inevitable aching back; and staying with it, when the fog clears, and the hot sun raises the field to a temperature beyond endurance.

Perhaps, because it is the climax of a two year cycle, harvesting the berries can be a period of celebration, or a time to get it done and over with, or an annual family duty, with its roots in time long enough that even the elders don't know when it started. Or like baked beans for supper Saturday night, salmon and fresh picked peas for July Fourth, or watching the New Year come in, it's something that has always been done at a certain time. My own reason is that I am an addicted berry picker. I would frequently stop in the heat of the day when the blueberries were too soft to rake, to pick wild raspberries in a cut-off on my way back to camp. But if raking the berries was the end of the cycle, it also heralded the beginning of another cycle. Stage one, to mow the field just raked, spread it with hay, and have it ready for the torch in April.

I began mowing with my Cub tractor the day after I had finished raking the 1981 berries. The north section went quickly, but I soon had trouble on the rough, rock strewn, back side of the southern section, that had been reclaimed from pasture. I broke a

Hay spread on a blueberry field. In the background are stacks waiting to be spread.

fitting that held the cutter bar in position. So on my way back to camp, I located Phil Durling, Jr. Phil, like most rural men, was something of a mechanic, and he had a portable welder. He met me at the lot next morning, his welder in his truck. It took far longer to position the broken part than it did for him to weld it. When it was neatly repaired, I asked him how much I owed. With a grin he replied, "I would charge any flatlander fifteen or twenty dollars, but you seem to be one of us and we tend to help each other. Give me six dollars." When neither of us could make change, I insisted he keep the ten I had. I do not remember that I ever had the opportunity to repay the favor, but always was, and still am one of them.

I again depended on getting hay from Carl Day. I hauled it the nine miles from Crawford to my blueberry field on a trailer back of my pickup about as fast as he mowed and raked it, I distributed it in small piles over the north field, having decided not to put off re-cycling the fields to annual crops, that I would accept the poor harvest, a second year burn on one field, in order to have a harvest every future year.

Bee hives are placed inside an electric fence to keep out the bears.

Mike, from across the road, who had helped with the raking, and with cutting and yarding pulpwood in the spring, began shaking out and spreading the hay as soon as I had hauled the first load. Between trips home, and one to Prince Edward Island, Canada, I hauled hay from Carl's to the blueberry field, staying at times to help Mike shake and spread it. I hauled the last load on September 24th and left most of it for Mike to finish spreading.

It was hardly an economical system, but I was retired, and considered the work an adequate sacrifice that allowed so much time for fishing in the nearby lakes.

Stage two of the cycle was the spring 1982 burn. The field, in early April, when family and friends had scheduled a weekend to help me burn, remained cold and wet. No one in the area had been able to burn. I stayed in Crawford, scythed bushes awhile each day, and rested (went fishing). Before leaving for home on April

22nd, I asked Paul if he and his crew would burn the north portion of my field. They did the next day. He charged forty-five dollars. It would have cost more to feed my family, had they come to do it. At home I had a letter from Gay Brothers that included a check for $369.66, with a note saying he had sold the berries from last year, for more than he expected, and was pleased to send me the additional amount. I wondered if he considered me one of them, or if it was to assure I would sell my berries to him in August. It certainly indicated they were honest.

In June, the patches of white seen in the fields were blossoms. I noticed that Guptill Farms had imported honeybees, a stack of four or more hives, piled at the corners of their fields, and there were other large fields with hives about town. The steady hum of bees could be heard yards from the edge of my field, and the air space was crowded as bees transported their precious cargoes across property lines. I remembered, and in following years I too took turns at renting bees.

I again had a small crew when my neighbors had secured all the available rakers. I was at camp the first week in August, and had loaded my winnower onto the pickup, along with a load of empty boxes and rakes. I went to the field the afternoon of the 5th and put out string. I raked about a bushel of berries to clear an area in which to back the truck into, and planned to do the winnowing on the pickup to avoid unloading and loading it daily, a system that worked very well.

Visitors, son Russ with grandson Brad, arrived on the 6th to fish. We had a heavy rain on the 6th. I raked two bushels on the 7th, but had trouble with the winnower belt, and took it to Guptill's for repairs. Jim and Big Russ arrived late, one fisherman and one raker! Mike, Jim, and I were the raking crew for 1981. It was a thin crop.

When Guptill Farms closed for the season on August 27th, we were nearly finished with the raking. The rest of the berries went to Gay Brothers, and I finished raking three days later.

The author's friend, "Big" Russ with a good catch.

CALENDAR OF BLUEBERRY TASKS

September
Mow weeds and bushes late in September; then haul and pile hay onto the land to be burned over next spring.

October and November
Spread hay on land to be burned over next spring, or burn over land to be burned with oil this fall.

December and January
Repair old equipment, and build any needed new equipment.

February, March, and April
Burn over land as soon as conditions permit.

April and May
Transplant blueberry plants as soon as frost is out. Apply fertilizer just as plants begin to grow. Keep watch for signs of cutworm injury and apply treatment if necessary. Dust for blossom and twig blight control.

May
Keep watch for flea beetle injury to the developing blossom buds; apply treatment if necessary. Apply treatment for thrips control on places where infestation was severe last year. Continue treatment for blossom and twig blight control.

May and June

Place honeybees on your land just as the blueberries start to bloom. Remove the bees before dusting begins. Continue treatment for blossom and twig blight control.

July

Apply treatment for weed control. Apply treatments for fruit fly control as announced by your county agent. Harvest available hay for use in burning.

August

Harvest and market the blueberry crop. Continue treatments for weed control. Harvest any additional hay that is needed for burning.

The Costs of Pruning with Different Methods*

Pruning techniques	10 acre	100 acre	1000 acre
Straw burning - manual spreading	148.89	123.43	119.64
Straw burning - mechanical spreading	211.08	98.97	85.94
Oil burning - conventional heads	236.31	112.74	98.68
Oil burning - Bosse' heads	225.43	77.65	61.17
Flail mowing**	34.77	16.40	16.16

* Includes equipment, labor and material costs as of June 1984 prices.
** 10A costs based on 16 hp tractor and one Mott mower; 100 acre based on 16 hp tractor and 2 Mott mowers; 100 acre costs based on 35 hp tractor and 3 Mott mowers.

Wild Blueberry Newsletter, September 1986

26

BLUE FIELDS

Nine years after I had obtained title to the blueberry land in Wesley, I felt that I knew enough about the industry to be qualified to at least manage a small field. I had not developed dependable crews to burn, or to rake, as had my neighbors who lived nearby. They depended on family and friends, and helping one another, if the need arose. My home, family, and friends were 260 miles away, making it very inconvenient for any of them to be available the day a field was ready to burn, or for the month needed to rake. In every tight spot in which I found myself, the locals came to my rescue.

My field was in full cycle, about half ready to harvest each year. I had acquired the tools necessary at the time to tame the Maine low-bush wild blueberry. They were: a bent piece of half-inch pipe with wick plugging one end to enhance the burning process; Indian fire pumps to help control the fires; blueberry rakes, buckets, and wooden half-bushel boxes in which to store the berries; a gasoline powered winnower; and a mowing machine. Each of these tools had been improved over the years. The mower had replaced the scythe, the winnower replaced the bean shaker, and some improvements had been made in the rake, but fire, a bent back, and wild berries had remained the same for a hundred years. An insecticide spray had been used since the blueberry fly epidemic of the early twenties, mostly on the barrens, but insects were less of a problem in the eastern part of the county. We saw an occasional maggot in my berries, but never to the extent that it was necessary to dust.

It was a routine agricultural pursuit, with the usual demons:

weather and market price. Both were favorable for the 1982 and 1983 harvest years. The processing plants paid growers 43 cents per pound in 1983.

The burning in 1983 was delayed because of weather conditions, but sons Jim and Russ, with neighbor Al Ecker came to camp and Carl Day and Steve Harrington, helped me burn the field on April 24th. It had not dried thoroughly, I was short of hay, and had spread none on a corner of the field. It was a poor burn. I took up four bales of hay from home the following weekend and spread it where I had missed before. The weather still unsuitable for burning when I left on May 3rd, I asked Paul Seavey to burn it when he burned a near-by field. Murphy's law dictated the results. Effect of the poor burn was compounded by a twenty cents per pound price, equaling disaster. Gross value of berries sold was $1017, more than $5000 less than either of the previous two years. It hardly paid for my gasoline to travel from home to Wesley, with my labor for naught. But family and friends enjoyed a good supply of free berries.

Billy Guptill told me that, working with a chemical company, he had field tested a herbicide spray that, applied after the burn, prevented growth of grass and most weeds without damage to the blueberry bushes. The advantage to the raker, not having the interference of grass while raking, and the possibility that fertilizers could be applied without encouraging increased grass and weed growth, indicated a break-through that would lead to other improvements.

Grower consideration included the cost of the herbicide, the cost of the machinery to apply it (or to have it done), and that once such fields were available, would a raker rake fields still with grass and weeds, even at a higher price.

The state required schooling and a license before anyone could apply the herbicide. The size of my field would not justify the investment necessary to purchase a tractor and spraying equipment. The alternative was to arrange with the buyer of my blueberries to spray the herbicide, which I, and others with more acreage than I had, also did.

I had recently hired Phil Durling to mow my field after the

harvest. The cost and risk involved in hauling my tractor, with mower attachment, from New Hampshire and back, using it only for one day, was not justified. The price of both services was an added cost to production, and with the mowing I had exchanged a labor income for the added cost.

The days of free blueberries, and the freedom to tame them, were about to meet new challenges.

Was it time to examine what we were doing, and the results of our efforts to tame the wild blueberry? I looked up the word tame in a dictionary: "rendered useful and manageable, change from the wild state, subdue." The description would apply to dogs, horses, cattle, chickens, but probably not to cats; it would apply to corn, beans, apples, and highbush blueberries, but lowbush blueberries, like cats, have not yet reached the full degree of description. Cats and wild lowbush blueberries, though they respond to attempts by humans to domesticate—the cat by being a pet, the blueberries by providing larger crops—are both capable of survival without human assistance. If you do not think a cat is independent, you have never kept a cat! They may be rendered useful and manageable, but never subdued. A pet dog, a farmer's cow, or his small flock of chickens, if left unattended would soon die. Without the food, water, medical attention (vaccines and antibiotics), and protection from wild animals and insects, they would soon become prey to one or more predators. In fact, once out of the barn or chicken house from which they might escape, they would do well to just survive the traffic when crossing the nearest road.

On an abandoned blueberry field—given over to natural forest seedlings, or seedling set to grow Christmas trees, or pulp wood—the berry rhizomes will remain dormant until the crop is harvested by man or fire, then sprout again, even many years later.

What is not in the definition is that taming also adds the responsibility to provide for what is tamed, except (for those mentioned) the cat and the wild blueberries were capable of survival in the wild without being provided for. However, the degree of taming for each also increases the degree of providing for what is required to maintain health and reproduction. If the word subdued is used here, it may be in a reversed role, the owner of the blueberry field becoming the servant.

The heavy concentration of bushes desired for maximum production of blueberries also provided a most desirable habitat for the blueberry fly in the early twenties, and for the black army cutworms in the forties. Each required service by the owner because of his responsibility to provide as he tamed. The natural burning resulting in pruning and increased production. When increased from occasional natural fires to burning after every harvest, it depleted soil humus, and required fertilizer for replacement of the nutrients. The herbicide to kill the grasses and weeds eliminated the fuel that had resulted in good burns, but that required purchase of hay or straw to replace the natural grasses that had fueled the burns.

I point out these developments in the taming of the wild blueberry, not only to record the commercial development of the process, but also to note the effect it had on those producing the product, and the effect it had on the lives of those involved. Blueberries were no longer free: services required were more and more becoming out of pocket costs, replacing what had been labor income for the farm and family.

Flail Mow Pruning

Last October, the Cooperative Extension Service conducted flail mow pruning demonstrations in conjunction with the University of Maine Agricultural Experiment Station and the U.S.D.A. The demonstrations showed how to flail mow, and we discussed the advantages and disadvantages of the practice. I have listed the advantages and disadvantages of flail mow pruning, and some of the things to remember when flail mowing. The cost of production tables listed below are updated for 1984.

Advantages

Flail mow pruning is an effective method of pruning lowbush blueberries and will cost less than burning. Traditional oil burning or straw burning can cost from $61.17 to $236.31 per acre, depending on the size of the farm and type of equipment used, whereas flail mowing costs could range from $16.16 to $34.77. Savings in production costs, labor and initial investment are additional financial benefits from flail mowing.

Blueberry News, 12/10/1984

27

DOUBLE PRODUCTION

Bill Guptill: "Through the '60s my father bought some other farms here in Wesley. A lot of the people living here were starting to move away, or to get older and could no longer take care of their farms. A lot of these people were relatives and we were given the first option to buy their lands. That is how we got more (blueberry) land at that time. We kept on increasing (production) by mowing the fields and fertilizing and grew more blueberries. We bought from Shirley Guptill, Alton Day, Harold Day, Bill and Nellie Hayward, Otis Carlow, Dick Sullivan and other local growers."

They kept on inventing equipment to sort berries, still in New York State, until Bill's father died in 1974, when he, his brother Charles (Skip), and mother Peg took over operation of the business and built processing facilities in Wesley that enabled them to ship completely processed berries to the storage facilities in Cohoes, New York

Bill Guptill: "...as we progressed along, in about 1978, we built our first blast tunnel that would blast-freeze the berries here (in Wesley). At first we were doing them almost fresh-pack and then freezing in New York State. Then we came up with a system of blowing cold air underneath them. They would ride on a current of air to go through the blast tunnel and would be frozen here, sorted, and then trucked to New York State once again in thirty-pound boxes. So each year we kept doing improvements."

Bill: "In about 1983 they invented a chemical (herbicide) called

Velpar and everybody's crop seemed to double by cleaning up (removing grass and weeds) fields, and each producer was growing more than they had before, so we had to go back to the plant (to expand to take care of the increase in volume of berries)."

The Maine Department of Agriculture report of Maine wild lowbush blueberry production for the years 1981 through 1985 best describes the effect of industry use of the herbicide Velpar. In millions of pounds for consecutive years beginning in 1981, it was 21,746; 35,925; 44,700; 24,680; and 43,700. Weather conditions for the year 1984 explain the low production statewide for that year. The increased volume also influenced the price. For the same years, the price paid growers in cents per pound was: 42.3; 52.0; 37.0; 25.0; and 23.0.

Guptill was still operating the processing plant for only about two weeks each year. Because the plant was so close (two miles) to my field, I continued to sell my berries to Guptill until they closed. Gay Brothers from Machias purchased the rest.

Now I was reminded of Billy Guptill having told me about the tests he had been running with the herbicide that eliminated the grasses and most weeds from a blueberry field. Velpar was a pre-emergence spray, applied before the plants sprouted in the spring and applied after the burn. It would be difficult and expensive for me to have prepared to spray my relatively small field, and training and a license was required for an applicator.

I asked Billy to apply the Velpar. He agreed to spray it, and he also suggested that fertilizer added in the spray would improve future crops. I complied. He was right. My harvest just about doubled following the first application. So did that of all other producers who had applied it.

Such drastic changes in production were sure to cause problems, and the first, of course, was to market twice as many berries. The industry, after a couple of difficult years, met the challenge through massive promotion programs and by developing foreign markets, though variations in weather conditions that affected the volume of production has from time to time influenced the market price.

The introduction of Velpar also influenced those who grew the

Bill Hayward operating a mechanical one-man raker.

blueberries. With only the berry bushes to prune (with no grasses or other weeds), the use of mechanical burners that did not require spreading of hay or straw, became more economical, and flail mowing was also more effective and became more popular. Meadow hay, and that from the few hay fields still available, was no longer needed for burning, and now the huge truckloads of straw for that purpose no longer arrived at dawn from Aroostook County and Canada.

Growers, particularly the large processing plants that owned hundreds of acres of blueberry land on the barrens, took another look at mechanical rakers. Charles Guptill had invented a riding, motor-driven mechanical raker many years before. Other inventors have since entered the field, and mechanical raking is no longer a prospect for the future. It is here now.

Charles Guptill never marketed his mechanical blueberry raker. At the time he built it, two and even three-year burns were being raked, and little attention or preference was given for original hay fields over original sheep pastures. The use of Velpar and fertilizer, which reduced the grass and weeds, and accompanying one year burn, not only increased the crops, it provided conditions where not only hand raking was much easier, but also made it possible to use mechanical rakers wherever the land was level and without rocks.

The barrens land was already mostly suitable for mechanical raking, as are the old hay fields that now grow blueberries in areas like Wesley. Models from hand-operated to large tractor-operated machines now in use will undoubtedly be improved in the years to come. The savings from not having to use itinerant rakers, and the elimination of arranging to have them there in time for a harvest, spells the end of hand raking as it once was.

However, those blueberry fields that once were pastures, picturesque with their assortments of rocks and holes left from long ago rotted stumps, cannot be raked with mechanical rakers. It would appear that such fields may well be on their way to planned obsolescence, unless they are reclaimed using expensive, heavy equipment to remove the rocks and level the fields. Hired rakers are already almost a thing of the past. Only those producers with family and/or friends and neighbors still willing to hand rake rocky fields will be able to continue that tradition. Perhaps there will continue to be room for hand raking for pick your own or organic fields.

BLUEBERRIES

With busy harvest done
It's back to school again
For some who raked the crop
The bending low to rake
Is not as far to reach
For growing boys and girls;
And those who earned the cash
Are apt to wear to school
The clothes they choose themselves.
There's always berries left
That some will fail to rake
By brush or pile of rocks,
By nest of angry bees,
By some who won't rake clean,
And sometimes berries spilled.
Now birds and porcupines
And bears and deer and ants
Will scrounge to clean the fields.

A truck load of baled straw.

Spreading bales of straw on the blueberry field.

28

CONTINGENT

Carl Day was in failing health and, thinking the value of his field would increase if he grew blueberries rather than hay, he stopped mowing and was burning his field by 1985. Guptill was already purchasing truckloads of straw from a broker in Canada. I called him and began getting a truckload (about 600 bales) from him each year. After they had been thrown off the truck, I distributed the bales of hay about the field with tractor and trailer. From there, Arnold and Stella Wood spread out the hay. At $1.40 per bale, I had reduced the amount used somewhat from what I had previously hauled from Carl's fields.

In so far as improving the burning process, there appeared to be no difference in using the straw rather than hay. There may have been some spread of foreign grass or weed seed brought in with the straw that burning and the herbicide spray did not kill—growers suggesting that to be the source of new weeds, but there were other sources, including seed used by road construction crews along roadsides, and lawn seed that included non-native grasses.

Tractor-hauled burners, fueled by propane or fuel oil, were being used more and more. They burned so hot that without hay or straw, the pruning was adequate, so cost was the only consideration.

With poor weather during the blossom period, and reports from the processors that much of the previous year's crop was still in storage, it looked like a bad year. For the first, and only time, I asked for a price guarantee, and Guptill offered .30 per pound. Jim and I started raking, but after two weeks, Guptill warned that they would be closing before we finished and suggested we get more rakers.

Neighbors were in the same predicament with no extra rakers. Paul Seavey expected to finish in a few days and offered to send a family of three to help. They arrived in a battered pickup truck, the back cluttered with assorted junk, and parked next to my winnower. It was late in the morning, when the berries were getting soft from a bright sun, more likely to jam in the rake. I mentioned that I hoped they could get started earlier the next day. They did not answer.

I gave each of them a rake that I had borrowed from Guptill, and assigned them to nearby ricks where the berries were thick, and went back to raking in a less productive area some thirty yards away, but near enough so that I could observe them. The man had selected the largest size rake; his wife and twelve year old boy had taken smaller rakes. The man swung the rake in a broad swath, the full width of the rick, more as if it were a scythe, with considerable strength, filling it with leaves, trash, and crushed blueberries, and then dumped the whole into his bucket. He took a step forward and took another broad swing with the same result. The boy attempted to copy his father's raking method with similar results. The woman turned her bucket upside-down, sat on it, and lit a cigarette.

The man quickly filled the first of his two buckets, and reached back for the second bucket, was ready to make another swing with the rake before I got up to where he stood. I suggested that he might take more care by using the rake properly, and certainly would not be crushing them so badly. He promptly told me he had been raking berries all his life, that he did not need me to tell him how, that perhaps he could give me a lesson or two, and furthermore, he would take no advice from me. Keeping in mind how badly I needed rakers, I backed off a bit, and reminded him that the berries were soft, that I would appreciate it very much if he would treat the berries a little more gently, and I went back to my rick.

He stood watching me until I was back to my buckets, then filled the second bucket by even more aggressive sweeps with the rake than before, the woman and the boy filling buckets in no less undesired manner. I made my way back up as he carried the two buckets over to the winnower. He saw me coming, lit a cigarette, before reaching for empty buckets.

I told him he would not need the buckets, because he was not going to rake any more of my berries, that I owned the field and the berries, and I would be the judge of how they could be raked, and who would rake them. I motioned for the woman and boy to bring their buckets over. I started the winnower motor, replaced a partly filled half bushel box of my own freshly winnowed berries with an empty box that would be filled with theirs, leaving mine under the edge of the winnower. They stood on the opposite side of the win-nower as I dumped their buckets into the machine, but I noticed that the boy, still holding his rake, had crawled under the end of the win-nower, and was still crawling along the ground toward the back of their truck. As he reached to put the rake in their truck, I reminded him that it was my rake, to bring it back. I remembered afterward that there was some conversation between the three of them, but I kept an eye on the boy and he brought the rake back around the end of the winnower and argued that it was his father's rake. I pointed out the blue paint on the rake, Guptill's identifying mark, and he passed it to me. I finished winnowing the berries they had raked, paid them by check, and waved them off my land.

I went back to my rick, glad to be rid of those rakers, and I decided I might find another place to sell my berries if I did not get them raked before the Guptill factory closed. My pails full, I brought them up to winnow. I bent to pick up my part filled box of berries before I started the winnower. The berries were a mush, crushed by the woman's feet as I winnowed their berries. I wished I had never seen that family, but thought myself lucky that I had caught the boy and prevented him from stealing the borrowed rake. It was not until I left for the day and collected the rakes to return the borrowed ones to Guptill that I learned that one was missing. It was the big one the man had been using. I then realized that the boy's action was to divert my attention while allowing the man to hide a rake without being seen.

I returned the rakes and paid thirty dollars for the one that had been stolen. I thought I might be able to stop payment of the check I had given them. The rakers would be passing Hanson's small grocery store, near my camp, on their way to where they lived. I stopped at the store, asked Dolly Hanson if they had cashed my check. They had. I would not leave Dolly, an old friend of many years, holding a cancelled check. She told me where they lived.

I drove up the road a few miles to a shack where the tramps were living. The junky truck was gone, but the woman was outside in the dooryard. I asked if she got her feet wet when she stomped on the berries in my box. She told me that I should not have left the box where people would be apt to step in it. I asked if she would like to return the rake they took, before I called the sheriff. She answered, "I don't have your rake. You can search the place yourself if you want. You won't find it." She was right, of course. I had learned a lesson.

One of the Gay Brothers, when riding by noticed I was still raking, and was pleased to purchase the rest of my berries after Guptill had closed.

Arnold and Stella Wood, and Lenny, having finished raking for Blanche Guptill, a few miles down the highway, and Blanche herself, all came to help finish raking my berries.

I did not let a low price, a small crop, or a miserable raker incident, spoil the harvest. I would liked to have been entertained by Princess, shared some berries with a black bear, or seen a deer through a morning fog, feeding near the edge of the field, but none of this came to pass that season. I was satisfied to be practicing the art of raking blueberries, passing the rake forward, under the berries, heeling the rake as I pulled it gently up and back, as the berries rolled back over the steel tines and into the storage part of the rake, then raised the rake over a bucket and poured the berries into it. So often on a foggy morning, the bushes wet, the sun of an August day would break through to dry and warm the field, and me.

29

SOME OTHER RAKERS

Few, if any, other rakers than my son Jim and I considered raking blueberries as an art, rather than a back-breaking way to earn a small amount of cash over a short period of time. This was particularly true of the school children of poorer families who accepted the fact that if they wanted something, perhaps even needed something, before school or for Christmas, that raking blueberries was the only way they would get it. It might be clothes for the girls and guns for the boys. There was also camaraderie among the young people while working on the fields that, though slowing the harvesting to some extent, tended to make for a more satisfied and genial crew.

The older, and those with many years of experience raking blueberries, tended to fall somewhere between the few who raked as an art and the few who scythed the field without respect for the product they harvested. For the most part, those owning fields depended year after year upon the same people, throughout generations of the same families, though they may have come from a nearby town or in some cases out from Calais or Machias. The owners depended upon them, and with their harvests occurring at the same time, each attempted to entice known better rakers, so as to get his harvest completed as rapidly as possible. Few of those passing by paid any attention to my marker-pencil cardboard roadside sign, RAKERS WANTED. After all, I was an unknown newcomer of a small field, with only two or three rakers working there—much less seductive than those more permanent signs posted by much larger fields, with twenty or more friendly rakers dotting the field.

I now had a market for my late-picked berries, but the earlier-picked berries were of better quality and weighed in heavier than the later harvest. The next year, Blanche and Stella again came to my rescue. Blanche was a recent widow who owned a fifty-acre blueberry field a mile away from mine. Stella had raked for her for many years. Blanche certainly did not need the added income, but I thought that after Blanche's berries were raked, Stella wanted to earn more money, and Blanche came with her, because they had always been friends. They were not children, perhaps fifty or so, with years of experience at shaking out the hay so as to improve the burning, as well as raking. They made no records as to number of bushels raked in a day, but they arrived early and quit when the berries got warm and mushed easily.

I do not think they thought of raking berries as an art, but it was like watching art in motion as, side by side, talking in low voices punctuated with occasional laughs, and with graceful motion (that made it look easy), they set their rakes and pulled them back and up, filled with clean firm berries.

Blanche, Stella, and her husband, Arnold, a part time truck driver, filled my need for rakers, other than family, for several years, and Stella continued to help after Arnold died, until she was no longer able to work.

I continued to be unable to attract early-season rakers, and had to depend upon rakers who were willing to rake more when they had finished with their first employer.

The following year, I was questioning natives about whom I could get to help with my raking.

Orris McKeown owned a twenty-acre field across the dirt road from my camp. On his field, the carpet of wild lowbush blueberries was white from blossoms in June, blue from ripe berries in August, and the foliage red in October. It was beautiful whether in harvest-cycle or not. One summer morning, I saw him out in the field with a pressure spray can in one hand and holding a two-foot length of black stovepipe in the other. He walked about, looking for weeds, and seeing St. John's Wort, or a Brown-Eyed Susan, a poplar, birch, or alder bush, he would slide the stovepipe over it so

Marge McKeouns on her field. Photo by Natalie Peterson.

as to keep the spray off blueberries and spray the weed-killer into the pipe, and look around for the next weed to eliminate. He had used this method of weed control for years and his fields were cleaner than most of weeds of every kind. He had turned over management of the field to his nephew's wife, Marjorie, who lived nearby, down by the lake.

Orris could well afford to hire someone to spray the weeds, but preferred to be there himself. He accepted the responsibility for care of the plants, and like feeding and petting a cat, he showed his respect for the wild plants. Not expecting to live to see any dollar return for his effort, he had to be motivated by his responsibility, while taming the berries, to care for them. It was the same reason why his niece, Marjorie, and Blanche Guptill, whenever they were in a blueberry field and saw a weed, stooped to remove it; the same reason that I, when picking broccoli, must remove a weed, though so near the end of the season it would have frozen before the seeds matured.

Full and empty boxes during the harvest at Marge McKeoun's field.
Photo by Natalie Peterson.

Orris was an old man, too old to rake blueberries, but from the
time when the blackened field showed its first spring green
growth, until the frost had killed all plant growth, he would be
walking slowly about the field. The diesel powered machines that
now spray insecticides and herbicides, that rake the berries, with
the operator riding high above the surface of the field, neither see
nor pull any weeds. When the plants and berries no longer came
in touch with human hands, for all their wildness something was
lost, became missing, like the mother's touch that's missing in too
many daycare centers.

It was a year when they would be harvesting a smaller part of
the field, and when Marjorie and a helper were putting out strings
to mark the ricks in early August, I asked her if any members of
her crew might want to work for me after hers were raked. When
her crew quit shortly after noon of their first day, Grace came to see
me. Grace lived in Woodland, eighteen miles to the north. If I
could use four rakers, a car full, they would help me when they
had finished with McKeown's. I told them to come.

Grace brought an older man, and his not so young school-teacher daughter who lived another twenty miles farther north on Route 1. They arrived early, well before the morning fog cleared. The fourth member of the crew was Grace's brother, Rick. Rick was a war veteran who had lost the lower part of one leg when a mine exploded under the truck he was driving. The wooden leg, apparently, was not usually comfortable, and he lost raking time by removing the wooden portion, displaying the stub with various comments while he changed the sock. While he managed to be entertaining the first day, his action became rather tiresome during later days, but Grace and the others were excellent rakers who more than made up for Rick's antics. They were my late crew for a number of years until the daughter fell and broke her leg, while trout fishing alone on a remote stream. It was not until much later in the day that she was missed, that parties set out to find her, and brought her in. Without a full car to share the cost of transportation, they did not return.

It reminded me that Olive Getchel, who had previously brought her young rakers to help rake my field, was also a trout fisherperson. She had taken her fish rod and walked up a stream near her home to catch a fish for supper. She died there and was found by the stream.

These were good people. They did not own the blueberry fields. To earn, by hard work, a few extra dollars, was not the major reason that they raked berries for me, particularly since they had already spent a week or two raking for someone else. I think they enjoyed, wanted to be a part of Blueberryland. The growers paid no tips at the end of the season, but one year, after a long, hot August day, I told each member of the crew to take their last half-bushel bucket of berries home with them. It made me feel good too.

30

PROGRESS

The mid to late 1980s continued, or increased my conflict between Atlantic salmon fishing, fishing on the nearby bass and white perch laden lakes, and tending to the increasing responsibilities of taming the Maine wild lowbush blueberries, which was now further complicated by increasing state and federal regulations. These regulations resulted in cost rather than labor income for the smaller producers like myself.

The increased problems of viral, bacterial, and fungal diseases, predators and poachers associated with concentrations of large numbers of a species, as with broiler growing, forestry plantings, and children in schools was inevitable. The resulting costs were felt by the processors, who were also feeling the increased costs due to regulations. Had proven mechanical rakers been available, the demise of hand rakers on the barrens may have taken place within a one-year period. Though delayed because of the investment cost, lack of the mechanical rakers available, and perhaps somewhat due to the knowledge that new and improved machines would rapidly become available, the struggle to reach the inevitable elimination of hand raking on compatible fields did not take place overnight.

Hand raking cannot compete economically with mechanical raking and will decrease as the quantity of berries needed to meet market demands will be grown on fields adapted to mechanical harvesting. During the mid and late 1980s my problems with getting rakers continued, at times increased. The Rideouts and the Rhodes families, from as far away as Woodland and Topsfield,

Jeff Guptill operating the mechanical raker.

filled my requirements for a few years. Only my son Jim and I raked the first week or more of the season for several years, and often depended on Stella and Blanche to finish the raking late in August.

The year 1986 was a disaster. It started when the field was too wet to burn when family and friends were available to come. I hired Jeff Guptill, and it was burned late with a propane burner.

Again, the Newfoundland salmon fishing trip took place the first week of August, and Jim and I started raking late, a week after the processing plant had opened. The state crop had doubled from the previous year, and the word was out that the price would be low following the huge increase in production due to starting the use of Velpar, which left freezers filled with unsold berries. My usual late-season rakers were still working at their own, or first fields.

I resorted again to asking Paul Seavey to influence his crew, about finished with his field, for help to get mine raked. His son was managing the crew of a dozen or more, and he agreed to bring them over. Seven arrived on the eighteenth, without the manager.

I put them to work without realizing that the crew included the same family of three with whom I had a previous problem. They were poor rakers; constantly used loud profanity and dirty talk, and were very undesirable rakers according to my standards. During a mid-morning break, they demanded a one-dollar a box increase in pay, which I refused. I paid them and they left, before I realized, though watching carefully, that they had stolen another rake and had tread into nine half-bushel boxes of berries, which they had stacked after winnowing, and which I did not find until I was loading them to take to the processing plant. That weekend I raked and filled 200 quart-baskets and trucked them home to sell at retail. Again, it was Stella, Blanche, and Steve Harrington who helped me finish raking the berries on August 28th. Phil Durling mowed the field.

I was more fortunate in other years. One year, my roadside RAKERS WANTED sign attracted two girls from Aroostock County who were riding by. They thought it might be fun—perhaps compared to picking potatoes—and promised to come back on the weekend, bringing their boyfriends. They came and were a big help. One year Marjorie McKeown convinced her whole crew, a dozen or more rakers, after they had raked her field across from my camp, to finish mine, which they did in three days. And another year, when Blanche had only a small field to rake, she brought her crew of five and my berries got raked much earlier than usual.

I recently visited with Blanche Guptill. She still lives in the house on Guptill Road to which she had moved when she became Dean Guptill's bride in 1928. Since Dean's death she has kept her blueberry fields smooth across the rolling hills, one back of her house, another near the cemetery where Guptill Road meets Route 192. They are mostly raked by mechanical rakers, by her son Jeff, who with his cousin, have recently cleared land that had once grown blueberries, but allowed to grow up. Now the considerable acreage is again growing blueberries. Jeff and his cousin are loggers who regard their blueberry acreage and the burners, sprayers, and harvesting equipment as a seasonal sideline to their skidders and trucks.

I asked Blanche why she and Stella came to my rescue so many times when I was unable to get rakers, and why they returned after the harvest to spread the straw on my land. Her answer was simple. She enjoyed being out in the fields, raking the berries, spreading the straw, and being a part of nature. Though now her fields are mostly raked by machines, she still has a few areas of rough ground where she hand rakes, and during the spring and summer, she visits the fields often, pulling a weed here and there, just enjoying seeing the bees work on the blooms, the berries set and turn blue, painting the field again.

She recalled the first years after moving there when a Micmac Indian family from a town east of St. Stephen brought their tents and camped on a corner of Gray's field, just across the road from their house. It was a large family, including great grandma to very young children. After their day of raking in one of Gray's several fields, they cooked their evening meal over an outside campfire, and at dusk, gathered around the fire. They brought out their fiddles, accordions, harmonicas, and drums and played and sang their native songs. Blanche and family and neighbors joined them. It was a wonderful experience.

The great grandmother wore a broad straw hat in the field and she chided Blanche for not protecting her eyes from the bright sunshine, for not providing protection from the heat of the sun. Then one day she brought Blanche a straw hat like the one she wore, that she had made, and gave it to Blanche.

In 1928, her husband Dean and his brother farther down the road sold their berries to Gaddis Brothers in East Machias, who for some years ran a canning factory. At that time Blanche remembered that they raked the berries in half-bushel baskets, and were paid seventy-five cents per bushel. After a few years Gaddis Bros. stopped canning berries but continued as a purchasing agent for Jasper Wyman Company. When Guptill built their processing plant, the berries were sold to Guptill Farms and still are. For some time before the Guptills had moved to Wesley, Dean managed their blueberry fields, burning and mowing the fields.

31

Time to Consider

In 1989, after ten years of active participation in growing Maine wild lowbush blueberries, it was about time to consider what changes had taken place, and what, if any, action was suggested as a result. It did not start off well. Our salmon fishing party arrived at our lodging on the Miramichi River in New Brunswick to find a fresh ten-inch snowfall on top of dirt roads turned to mud from a previous, short warm spell. Four- wheel drive vehicles got us from the road to the cabin on the bank of the river. We cast for salmon in the open water between floating ice cakes. Resting, during a warm-up period, I stepped out of the cabin to the edge of the river-bank to watch a friend play a salmon, slipped, slid into a cement post at the foot of an eight-foot bank, and broke my hip.

The limited activity period that followed provided time to review my ten years in the blueberry business. It also reduced my labor-income participation to some extent.

I recalled the early days when family helped burn the field, and family raked most, sometimes all, of the berries. I mowed following the harvest, and hauled waste hay from a neighbor and spread it on the field. Taxes, now more than doubled, and my transportation from home to Maine were the major out-of-pocket expenses. Total expenses in 1990 were $4927.71. That included $834.75 for straw, $485.00 to spread it, $182.00 to mow, $783.00 to spray herbicide and fertilizer, $380 to burn, $1613.75 to rake. Ten years before, all of these activities, if required, had been accomplished by myself and family members...labor income for the family. Now it was cash to be paid first from the sale of berries.

Ten years before, sale of berries was $4232.00, in 1990, $4591.47. That was an increase of $360 in sales for an increase in cost of $4278.50. That, of course, is not an accurate average annual difference, but it does show the trend. Annual variations in price received per pound (from .20 to .60), and volume of berries (2000 pounds to 25,000 pounds) occurred during the period, the range clearly indicating the feast or famine risk of agriculture.

What had brought about such a change?

The do it yourself to maintain family labor income rather than an out-of-pocket cash expense became untenable when the last one-horse mower (or cub tractor) in town broke down, and the processing plant, or a large land owner, purchased a modern tractor with mower available for hire. The small landowner could not afford such equipment to do his own one day a year of mowing, and the owner of the equipment needed more work than his own to afford the equipment.

Straw had to be purchased because the hay fields had been turned into blueberry fields and the grasses in them killed by herbicides. In addition, spraying required special and expensive machinery and a tractor capable of operating it, and it had been shown that insecticide spray was often necessary to produce a marketable crop, that herbicide spray increased the crop, as well as greatly increased raking speed, and that fertilizer was becoming necessary to replace what was being taken out of the soil. Only the large landowners had use for such a sprayer for enough hours use per year to pay for it. For their smaller producers, the processors made their equipment available...at a price.

On the whole, the management programs maintained, or increased production and profit, but in doing so they made it impossible for the small blueberry field landowner to survive as a totally independent self-reliant unit.

The alternative was to lease the field to a processor, or a very large landowner, who had enough land to justify the expensive equipment, as well as adequate office staff to keep up with and follow the ever-increasing government mandates, which included everything from calculating social security taxes for alien

(Mexican) rakers, to figuring the legally acceptable concentration of an herbicide spray and the steps required to license an applicator, to arranging for how many portable public toilets were required per acre. I still have not figured out, according to the federal agricultural forms recently received, if I, or the man who leases my field, is the sharecropper.

Had I been younger, I might have looked into what regulations apply to a pick-your-own blueberry field, or perhaps reverted to harvesting only free untamed berries, marketing them as organic.

After more than fifty years of operating their blueberry business in Wesley for two weeks every August as a part of their Cohoes, New York business operation, the Guptill brothers, William (Bill) and Charles Jr. (Skip) divided the company, with Skip keeping the Cohoes enterprises and Bill operating the rapidly expanding blueberry business.

At the time of my decision to lease my blueberry field, Bill was not interested in taking on another field. After due consideration I leased the field to Herbert Hanscom of East Machias.

Machine Harvesters

This was to be the year two new machine harvesters were introduced to Maine growers. As it turned out the NIMCO Harvester was not ready for demonstration until mid-September, and the Bragg Lumber Company machine was only available for demonstration one of the two times scheduled. However, those who came to the demonstrations were able to see the Darlington harvester (converted cranberry rake).

The harvesters seem to do a particularly good job in fields that have a small crop. In fields with big crops, a machine will not pick up a long string of blueberries lying on the ground, whereas a good hand raker will. Work will continue on perfecting the machine harvesters and determining the best field conditions for them to work in.

Wild Blueberry Newsletter, October, 1985

32

HERBERT HANSCOM

There are nine plants in Maine that process wild lowbush blue-berries, all in Washington or Hancock Counties, with six of them close to the high-producing barrens. The logistics involved with the supply of this seasonal product has developed over the years largely by way of the experience, ingenuity, and magic of many unique individuals.

Herb Hanscom is one such individual. He grew up with blue-berries, and has participated in every phase of the industry from raking as a school child, to growing and harvesting his own field, to winnowing and burning, to getting his own and other growers' berries to a processing plant. He has personally experienced the expansion and management changes that have taken place in every aspect of the industry, as a hired-hand, as a producer, and also as a buyer for a processing plant—each of those roles an important part of this very integrated business.

With my son, Jim, I recently interviewed Herb and his wife at their home in East Machias.

WS: "I am interested in when you started with blueberries. How did it happen that you got interested in blueberries, and what happened as you got more and more into it, and your feeling about it as it happened?"

Herb: "I suppose that my very first connection with blueberries was, as children, probably very young teenagers, we started pick-ing blueberries."

WS: "Picking or raking?"

Herb: "Both. There was a time when they couldn't be sold to any great extent. The market wasn't very good and there was a lot of hand picking going on. They were put into quart baskets and then crates of either 24 or 36 quarts and then shipped to the New York market."

WS: "What years would that be?"

Herb: "Probably in the first of the 30s...36. And we were paid—there were a few adults that did this too because those were hard times back then—we were paid five cents a quart to pick those by hand. That was my first experience with blueberries. Then, as soon as the market got a little better for raked berries, hand picking sort of phased out and we raked berries for various people. The first of our raking we got thirty-five cents a bushel, two half-bushel boxes. The grower got $1.15 a bushel. They were canned at that time. There weren't any freezers."

WS: "Were you born on a farm that had blueberries?"

Herb: "Yes, a small amount. My father's farm probably raked about 100 bushels a year. Then we'd work for a neighbor."

I told Herb that in *The History of Wesley* it was stated that Went Leighton was the first in that town to grow blueberries.

Herb: "That is the first fellow I raked for. Went Leighton, and that field is right where the tower is, not the old tower, but the one they just built...he had a camp there for himself, and he had a tent area for his rakers. That was the first place where I raked blueberries; at that time, I think there was a little collection of us from down here. After I got out of high school we raked up there, and we raked real late into the fall. After we had all of his bushes raked, we raked for Thatcher Guptill, and then we raked for Roger Gray. Roger had the George Day place right across the road from us (Leighton). That's the place where we stayed in a tent and raked with mittens on."

After being drafted and completing his term in the service, Herb returned to Maine and started hauling berries for the Medomac Canning Company of Rockland, which bought berries from the locals in Wesley.

Herb: "I graduated to doing work on their land, burning,

Flo Hanscom, center, and workers cleaning from the conveyor belt.
Photo by Natalie Peterson.

mowing. Then the fellow who looked after their business in this
area retired and he recommended me. I worked for Medomac in
that capacity for about fifteen years. They had a receiving station
down here, and we transported the berries to Rockland until the
canning seemed to phase out and freezing took over. Then we
took the berries into Portland to Northeast Cold Storage and to
Cumberland Cold Storage. They did the cleaning, freezing, and
storage, but Medomac still owned the berries. It was up to them
to find the market for them. Then there were some bad years. The
price was down to ten, eleven cents per pound—and the final
blow, I guess, was when the principal owner of Medomac
Canning developed cancer. The bank called in his loan and the
company went through bankruptcy. That was in the early '80s....
So then I was out of a job as far as blueberries went, but that lasted only about a month or two until about half of the customers
that had been selling to Medomac came to me and said they
would like to have me take care of getting rid of their berries; that

Flo Hanscom. Photo by Natalie Peterson.

is, selling their berries for them. That's when I became associated with Allen's and I've been there ever since in the same capacity. I bought berries, leased land and sold berries to Allen's."

Herb recounted his experiences growing berries on land he had purchased or leased; they were very similar to my own. He talked about first spreading hay, then straw, to burn after mowing, then changing over to gas or oil burning; and about the gradual additions of fertilizer and insecticides. He mentioned that the early herbicide also killed blueberry bushes; so to keep the poison off the blueberry bushes, it was applied from a roller on back of a tractor. The roller would be suspended above the height of the blueberry bushes, so that it would paint the leaves of the taller weeds. However, this herbicide would not kill the birch, alder, or poplar, so either another herbicide was applied with a brush by hand, or else they were just cut back. I recalled that the Gay Brothers once applied that method on my field.

Herb: "The first time I saw Velpar, one of our big growers managed to get a little of it the year before it was approved. He used it on three or four acres. Just before picking time, he invited a lot of us who were interested, to come and take a look at what it had done. It had done a beautiful job, and it appeared—because the competition (grass and weeds) had been cleaned up—that it would increase his crop by probably 50 percent. I had gone to look at it with an older fellow who raised a lot of berries around here. We looked at it and he said, 'You know, this might be the best thing that ever happened, but it might be the worst.' I guess you could take it either way. There was an awful change in the yearly production all over the area. Where a normal crop had been 28-30 million pounds, it began to change dramatically, up to 40-50 million.

I would be guessing that was probably about 1980. We have now got up to 100 million pounds and it's become a big challenge to market that many.... Right now, they are estimating that when they start to harvest again this coming year (2001), there will be roughly 30 million pounds left on hand. That is sort of a softening-up to get us prepared for another reduction in price."

Among other entrepreneurial activities, Herb Hanscom operates a Christmas wreath production plant of considerable size each fall. He also packages, sells, and distributes fresh Maine wild blueberries in ten-pound packages and in attractive pint baskets. His wife, Flo, takes an active hands-on part in the neat processing plant.

Oxford County Extension Blueberry Meeting
Sponsored by the Maine Cooperative Extension Service

Date:　Wednesday, March 20, 1985
Place:　Country Way Restaurant, South Paris

Agenda

10:00 - 10:45　　Increase Profits With Fresh Marketing,
　　　　　　　　Panel Discussion
　　　　　　　　Harold "Bud" Brown, David Carter, Steve Cummings,
　　　　　　　　LeRoy Phinney and Frank Bucknell

10:45 – 11:00　　Maine Agricultural Promotion Assistance
　　　　　　　　Matching Grant Fund
　　　　　　　　Representative of Maine Dept. of Agriculture,
　　　　　　　　Food and Rural Resources

11:00 – 11:15　　Pick-Your-Own-Basics, A Marketing Alternative
　　　　　　　　Tom DeGomez

11:15 – 11:45　　Blueberry Commission's Marketing Activities
　　　　　　　　Ed Piper
11:45 – 12:00　　Pesticide Container and Drift Law*
　　　　　　　　Bob Batteese

PART V: REVIEW

Burned over blueberry field showing rocks that have to be removed before a mechanical harvester can be used.

33

THE LAND

He who leased my blueberry land these last ten years has doubled the production and maintained the field in better condition than I was able to do. But with variation in yield from sixteen to two tons on the same land in subsequent harvest years, erratic weather, and prices varying from 20 to 60 cents per pound, realizing a profit that one can depend upon continues to be a challenge, which neither he nor anyone else has been able to overcome.

In order to conform to changes in equipment used and in management practices, land improvement has become necessary. The use of mechanical, bottled gas, or fuel oil-fired burners has eliminated the need to mow the field following harvesting, as well as the need to purchase and spread hay or straw in order to generate enough heat to properly prune the bushes.

Mechanical rakers, from hand-operated units to large tractor-driven rakers that reduce harvest time by days, if not weeks, are now available and being improved with each season. However, mechanical rakers require smooth level fields on which to operate.

Many of the old hay fields are dotted with out-croppings of ledge, large rocks, or piles of smaller stones, which mowers, swinging scythes, even horse-drawn mowing machines, would simply go around. Over a period of many years, rocks of considerable size "grew up" from the ground due to frost action. The old pastures, which became blueberry fields, are littered with rocks of various sizes and pitted with the holes left from burned and rotted stumps of large trees. The rugged terrain is no impediment for those raking by hand. In fact, it seems that the berries grew bigger

Rocks removed from the author's land.

and thicker around the old stumps. But the mechanical rakers cannot be used on such land.

Landowners recognized that, as more and more fields became mechanical raker accessible, it would become more and more difficult, and more expensive, to continue production on such property. It meant that rocks must be removed, and the holes leveled. Many of the blueberry fields, including my own, consisted of part old-field, with occasional rocks or rock piles, with the rest of it being acreage that had been pasture, with huge rocks, the remains of stumps, and potholes. During recent years, bulldozers, backhoes, and logging trucks with loading equipment have been seen during the off-season in many blueberry fields, and the rocks removed have provided for new stone walls around many old pastures

There was more original pastureland than hay field on my own land. With a favorable crop and price during recent years, I have invested in rock removal. Despite the hourly cost of equipment required for excavation and removal, the profit on the harvest has been enough that a larger pile of rocks has accumulated off the field than what was previously observed in the field. Then there is the matter of the holes left behind. If the ground were to be leveled, which means uprooting the bushes, it will take several years before the rhizomes spread back over, which means a temporary reduction in the harvest.

Smaller families, child labor laws, and hiring competition (ask any teenager if he or she would prefer to rake blueberries or work at McDonald's), have seriously reduced the numbers of young rakers, and there is less incentive for older individuals to rake. Government agencies, looking for work for crews of itinerant Mexican laborers, between periods of picking string beans and apples, have brought them to the blueberry fields.

There came a year, when a change in manufacturer of fertilizer and/or herbicide, or its application, and weather conditions resulted in a partial kill of blueberry plants and an infestation of weeds (Brown-Eyed Susan and St. John's Wort) that seriously reduced production from my field. The weeds also interfered with raking. The harvest was considerably reduced; the discouraged rakers left broken buckets, fast food wrappers, and beer cans to litter the field.

The extreme drought during July and August of 2001 undoubtedly reduced the amount, berry size, and quality of an expected record crop of Maine lowbush blueberries, except on the relatively small acreage where it was possible to irrigate. Changing its habitat from rock-strewn mountainsides to level fields, providing methods of protection from its insect and fungus enemies, removing competition from natural vegetation, and fertilizing with chemical nutrients to replace the natural plant food depleted as a result of the forced increase in berry production, the industry continues the effort to tame the wild lowbush blueberry. It also enforces obsolescence upon a way of life that, though still remembered by but a few, is already a part of history.

34

INDUSTRY GROWTH

I asked Bill Guptill to summarize the mechanical and chemical innovations that produced the increase in lowbush blueberry production over the years.

Bill: "I'd have to blame a lot of that on my father, because back in 1937 through 1947, he built six mechanical harvesters, trying different styles. He had five different types built to perfection and tried to use them here in Wesley. His main goal was a better way to pick blueberries. He started in those early years trying to make it better, but at that time nobody really cleared up his or her land. One part of the field, all rocks might be gone, but then in the pasture.... The land so rough the machines could not operate properly. He tried to make equipment that duplicated the motion of hand raking and he was very successful. The machines built today—I am not saying they copied—but they certainly look an awful lot like different units my father built in those years. He showed them off at the Cherryfield Fair one year.

"At that point he started working very hard cutting and cleaning up his blueberry land. He would mow and rake immediately after we had harvested the blueberries so there would be no seeds (from grass and weeds) to compete with more blueberries growing in. Then he would try different experiments—that was on this piece of land here—such as spreading sulfur (fertilizer). Wesley had old blueberry fields, and even when I came along after dad passed away, in running around here as a young boy, I remember that a lot of those fields that had been blueberry fields originally

Guptill's processing plant.

had grown up (to bushes, trees) at the time that we bought them. We went back in and cleaned up, and cut off all the trees, and started to mow and burn."

WS: "What had made them stop growing blueberries, those who had let it happen?"

Bill: "I think it was probably two-fold. Everybody in Wesley, the way it looked to me, seemed to give his or her children a good education. A lot of them became schoolteachers and got other positions and moved away, which left the original family at home. The original family members just kept getting older, and the younger generation had their own lives to live and didn't seem to have an interest in blueberries and did not come back. Blueberries were not enough, and if you had a regular job, it was more important to keep that regular job than to come back and rake blueberries. So a lot of the old blueberry fields were left to grow up. Where the land was reasonably in good shape, not real rough, like for instance the Brooks field; that was all cleared at one time. When we bought it, it probably had fifteen years of growth (brush and trees) on it that we had to clear, to get thirty acres back. We did it the hard way, cutting every individual tree, putting each of them through a chipper. Since then there have been many changes.

"The bush hogs have gotten better, so they can clean up land for you. Today we have equipment that has power heads that we can start at the top of a tree and actually chip it all the way right down to the roots. There is a stump grinder that will take away the stump. After we let it set for a year and get back and burn it, you would never know it wasn't blueberry ground right along. But it takes a long time. A blueberry bush grows only an inch a year, so the bare spots have to grow in from the patches all around. When you clear a piece it takes years and years to get the amount of blueberry bushes that were there originally.

"We were exceptionally lucky here that as we cleaned up this land, the blueberry bushes grew in. It was a special bonus when the chemicals (herbicides) came along about 1983. It cleaned up all the grasses and the brush was gone. We did not start to notice exactly how good it was going to be until years later. The blueberry bushes had to be re-stimulated to start to grow, because the forest had shaded them for so long.

"Through that time period we learned a lot about bees and how important pollination was. Today we know that for each hive of bees you have, you can get an extra thousand pounds of berries to the acre. If you bring in four hives your potential is four thousand pounds to the acre. Wesley has a lot of woods land around (the blueberry fields) and we have a lot of natural bees and bumblebees and other things. Wesley is not like the barrens. We had a lot of other pollinators and bugs that would come out (of the woods) and do a lot of our pollinating.

"Here in Downeast Maine we would always be cooler than the barrens. Back in those years we used to get a lot of fog. In later years we don't get the fog we used to get twenty years ago. It was not unusual to be fogged-in in Wesley for two weeks straight in the middle of August. The last ten years I can't tell you when we were fogged in for a day. There was always dew in Wesley in the morning. Now, lots of time there is none. I don't know if that is global

Frozen berries flow into totes for storage. Photo by Natalie Peterson.

warming or the jet stream, but there is a difference in Wesley's climate at this point.

"Many things have happened in the fields to make them better. It made it easier on the rakers, having cleaner fields. The product that comes in from the fields now no longer has the squashed berries and things from having alders out there to rake through. It really improved the quality of the berries 100 percent. We started to get a much better berry—not that any rakers are actually happy no matter what's there. Good rakers…many years ago would maybe get eight to ten bushel a day, and today you get rakers that get fifty to sixty bushels raking in the fields. The record is about two hundred boxes (100 bushels).

"So then, as the years went on, it seemed like we added on every single year, because we either got a few more berries that we bought locally or our berry crop increased…and we kept adding on. Then finally, in about 1992, I put up the storage freezer here where we froze everything. The berries would stay here and we

Cleaning and washing line. Photo by Natalie Peterson.

Rocks removed from Guptill blueberry fields. Now stonewalls sur-
round the property

could store about eight million pounds, then truck them to New
York State to be sold. Or, the international market was getting to
where they were buying blueberries in Europe, so we were shipping to Europe and other countries."

WS: "Are you still cleaning, freezing, sorting and packaging
the berries now as you were doing when you bought my berries?"

Bill: "For many years, until about 1992, we would continue to
box them during the month of August and be done with them
here, but then the blueberry business became a separate business
from New York and I moved down here to stay. Then we built the
freezer so we would have a place to put the product. In 1992 we
put them into tote bins, which are 1200 pounds of blueberries in a
single plastic-lined, cardboard carton. At that point we would put
them in the freezer here and bring them back out for sorting. We
also bought a color sorter that would individually take a camera
image of the blueberries and any as green berries went through, it
would shoot air to move the green berries or moss or foreign
objects ahead one half inch because they were not the same color

as a blueberry, so the good berries would drop down separately. So at this point we started using color separation followed by the girls for a final check-over on the tables. The blueberries are stored in the freezer storage in the totes until taken out to fill orders and put them into the 30s (pound boxes).

"The difference is, through the years, Europe might want a different pound box than we do. We do 5s, 10s, as well as 30s. There are many different size boxes."

Velpar (Hexazinone) Registration:

The herbicide, Velpar, is now approved for use for weed control in lowbush blueberry fields in Maine. Velpar is effective in controlling a wide range of weeds that are common in lowbush blueberry fields. Some of the weeds controlled with Velpar are: grasses; flowering, herbaceous weeds (such as: hawkweed, asters, blackeyed susan, goldenrod, pearly everlasting, fireweed, cinquefoil, and dogbane), and woody weeds (such as: hardhack, wild rose, cherry, sweetfern, poplar and lambkill). As a result of reduction in weed competition, blueberries have more light, water and nutrients available to them. They respond by increasing stem numbers and the number of flower buds per stem. This, in turn, results in a significant increase in blueberry yield.

Blueberry News, 5/5/1983

35

CAUTION

The responsibility for using the various insecticides, fertilizers, fungicides, pollinators and herbicides to improve the blueberry crop is divided between the manufacturer of the product; those who determine its need, time of and approved use; and those who mix and apply it.

It is probably unavoidable that over a period of time, one or more of these applications will be inaccurately mixed or applied, or that the conditions under which they are used will not have been adequately tested. It was reported that an herbicide application might have damaged some of Guptill's land. It appears that such a problem may have occurred in the treatment of a small section of my own land.

I asked Bill Guptill: "What about the blueberry land now? You mentioned some of the problems you had with your land. What is the story there now?"

Bill Guptill: "My land has really been set back for many, many years to come."

WS: "The problem related to the use of an herbicide?"

Bill: "It actually killed the blueberries (bushes)."

WS: "Did it damage the land for other use?"

Bill: "Well, there is really no other use for blueberry land at this point. So really, I am back to the scenario—starting back 100 years ago—of having the land come back in, trying to use as many cultural practices that I can to enhance it to grow (blueberries). We are using mulches to try to get it to restart. It actually killed all the bushes and vines."

WS: "How do you get berries to come back in? Will they come back in eventually (naturally)? Is the damage still in the ground?"

Bill: "The damage is probably now gone from the ground. This happened back in 1996. We are still seeing a decline of the blueberry bushes. I should say that it was 1996 and 1997 that I put it on, and we are still seeing declines, but hopefully this year we're hoping to see the destruction level off, at least start to stand still, but there are so many vines gone that it is really hard to get a raker to go out and hand rake a little patch of blueberries or go around the side of the field (where it was not applied). Even for a machine it is very hard to go out and pick out there now because you can be out there all day for ten boxes of blueberries. There's just not the volume there that once was there. And we're hoping to bring them back. That's our main goal. A blueberry—there's nothing I can do to make it grow faster than an inch a year. However, it took hundreds of years to get here in the first place and I imagine it will take a hundred years to get them here again."

WS: "Were there other people's fields that got damage like that too? What about the fields you were spraying?"

Bill: "There are other fields that have trouble, or they have been cut out or not raking as much as they once did. It's just a problem that will take a lot of time to heal and grow back.... The University of Maine has been great. David Yarborough (Extension Blueberry Specialist) has been excellent. He has done more than his share of helping me out with what to do."

I talked with David Yarborough about the cause of the problem, of why it occurred in some fields and not in others. His explanation from their findings is that on the esker type land—sand and gravel areas where drainage is deep and rapid—the chemical disperses rapidly. However, in fields where the subsoil is too near the surface and dense, the chemical will remain within the root range of the blueberry bushes until a second application even two years later, may result in an accumulation strong enough to kill the bushes.

It appears probable that in an effort to kill sweet fern growth in one area in my field, that enough of the chemical remained long enough to severely reduce blueberry growth. Inspection by individuals trained to recognize problems in blueberry fields will undoubtedly identify varying degrees of damage that have not previously or accurately been diagnosed in many fields.

Asked about establishing new fields, Bill explained, "They are there in the forest. Berries need a very low pH soil, 4.5 to 5.0 is probably optimum. You need that to start with and they seem to grow where nothing else does, on ledges, under rocks. They seem to be in the worst fields. You could not mow it. Virtually everyone has picked up rocks and moved them to the sides or thrown them off the fields, and a lot of old timers before we came along picked up many rocks. You see the rock piles that are back in the woods and the rock piles in the middle of the fields. They did a tremendous amount of work before any of us started to pick out rocks. You can still see in the fields a lot of marks where they took chisels out to drill holes in the rocks so that the frost will blow them apart, leaving remnants of them that we see as we pick rocks from the fields. They did a lot of work before we ever did one thing.

"I think a lot of it is a patch gets going, a bird comes along and eats some berries and then does its thing and actually plants the seed that starts the bushes. The seed has to pass through some digestive system, but they've got bear, deer, and everything going, and they all eat blueberries and go out and go to the bathroom all over the woods. If the soil is right, and they get enough light, they will start to grow underneath a complete forest. After you clear that forest you will see that they come in real quickly. A lot of land I clear today is land I walked through and even though it had not been blueberry field, you can look down and see those nice little bright red sprouts individually there. After we burn that and clean it up, in a couple more years they'll start to grow in abundance."

I mentioned that when I first came to Wesley, old timers told me that to get blueberry bushes to grow in bare patches in a field, they would stick a branch into the ground like it was a small tree, for the birds to perch in, so that they would plant blueberry seed. I asked Bill if he thought it actually helped grow bushes in the bare spots. He agreed that it probably did.

36

BLUEBERRY HILL FARM 2001

High fences mark the land in both directions from the office of Del Emerson, Superintendent at Blueberry Hill Farm, along a stretch of Route 1 in Jonesboro. The fences were to keep out man and beast poachers, and to prevent vandalism from disrupting the many on-going research experiments in constant progress.

Mr. Emerson grew up during the late days of the Depression on a farm at the edge of the barrens in Columbia, one in a family of ten children. He was picking blueberries by the age of seven, and lived with and worked with blueberries as the industry developed. The move to manage Blueberry Hill Research Farm in 1953 was only a few miles, and his experience well-fitted him for the position.

With a wistful look he recalls those early days of the blueberry fly disaster and the period of time when, picking wild blueberries, like hunting deer, and catching trout, was an accepted necessity of living off the land. He had taken his rod to one of those memorable streams, only the day before I talked with him, but he had returned without a fish. He recalled how the barrens have changed. The tall pines have been cut so as to allow the helicopters to hover closer to the field when spraying. There is no longer cover for the deer that were once so plentiful, and birds can find little protection in the great open spaces. The blueberry plants are still there, and in greater numbers, aided by spraying to kill the insects and fungus, fertilized to return nutrients that the massive crops take from the soil, cross-pollinated by hives of bees set on the edges of the fields, irrigated when nature fails to provide enough rain to result in big

Research fields at Blueberry Hill Farm.

full berries, harvested by mechanical rakers which have replaced the school children and whole families of hand rakers. Though we still call it wild, the Maine lowbush blueberry is at least corralled, tamed, and protected from its natural enemies.

Del Emerson needs no more recommendation than that he has remained on the job since he was first hired in 1953. It is the only wild blueberry research farm in the country. It continues to carry out the research requirements needed by industry. It is part of the University of Maine Cooperative Extension Service, which brings the results to the blueberry growers.

There is always need for more testing: Is a new mechanical raker safe to use? Does it rake more of the berries with less damage? Does it rake faster?

A new herbicide is available that will kill weeds not killed by previously used herbicides: What is the correct and safe concentration? Does it remain in the soil? Is it harmful to man or beast?

What kind of bees, and how many are needed for maximum pollination? How best can blueberry plants be encouraged to fill in bare spots in a field? Whenever a new insect appears on the scene, someone must determine which insecticides and methods of use will work best. And, naturally, whenever a field problem presents itself, the pressure is on to find an immediate solution.

Visitor information booth at Blueberry Hill Farm. Photo by Natalie Peterson.

The measured spaces beyond the fences, plots marked by flags, or otherwise, identify tests in progress, some that may be completed in a year, others in two, three, or more years. All are of importance to blueberry growers, from the smallest to the largest.

Del commented on the increasing influence and importance of the Canadian—particularly in Nova Scotia and New Brunswick—government and grower's expansion and participation in wild lowbush blueberry production. It has taken an active and successful sales promotion to market the rapidly increasing production of these blueberries, and that volume of production, supported by the research and experiments conducted by the University and the testing at Blueberry Hill Farm, will require continued effort to market.

37

WILD BLUEBERRY COMMISSION OF MAINE

From the Maine Extension Service Bulletin:

Purpose and Goals of the Wild Blueberry Commission of Maine
The mission of the Wild Blueberry Commission of Maine is to provide the foundation upon which Maine's Wild Blueberry growers and processors can build profitable businesses. Title 36, section 4301 states the purpose as:

> The production and marketing of wild blueberries is one of the most important agricultural industries of the State, and this chapter is enacted into law to conserve and promote the prosperity and welfare of this State and of the wild blueberry industry of this State by fostering research and extension programs, by supporting the development of promotional opportunities and other activities related to the wild blueberry industry.

The full statute related to both the Wild Blueberry Commission of Maine and the Wild Blueberry Advisory Committee is available from the Maine Extension Service.

Organizational Structure
The Wild Blueberry Commission of Maine serves the priority needs of Maine's Wild Blueberry growers and processors. The Commission appoints the Wild Blueberry Advisory Committee to set research priorities and make research recommendations. This

committee also works to obtain research grants and supports the grant writing of wild blueberry researchers.

The Commission achieves its promotional objectives through the Wild Blueberry Association of North America (WBANA). Annually, the Commission makes grants to fund WBANA's operating plan for Wild Blueberry promotion.

The Commission employs a full time executive director to plan and execute other activities of the Commission, provide staff support to the Advisory Committee, and to administer the business of the Commission. Currently, the Commission provides administrative staff support to the executive director.

Maine Blueberry Commission

On October 30, 1985, the Maine Blueberry Commission met in Ellsworth. One of the major topics was budgeting the estimated $450,000 blueberry tax revenue from the 1985 crop. This the second year that the tax has been one cent per pound (one-half cent for processing plus one-half cent for growing). Of the $450,000, approximately $100,000 will go to support the UMO research and Extension programs, and $70,000 will be used for instate promotion and for operating expenses by the commission. The remaining $280,000 was earmarked for promotional activities outside the state, primarily with the Wild Blueberry Association of North America and the North American Blueberry Council.

Wild Blueberry Newsletter, November 1985

38

HIGHBUSH BLUEBERRIES

Highbush blueberries are a major factor in the total production of blueberries in the United States. However, with only twenty growers, totaling less than 100 acres, all in the southern counties, Maine production has no commercial influence. They are mostly produced in New Jersey and Michigan.

The commercial varieties were originally taken from wild bushes during the 1920s, and have been selected and crossed for size and flavor of the berry, as well as adaptability of the bushes to soil and weather conditions. Only one commercial variety was selected from those native to Maine, and varieties originating from warmer climates are more susceptible to freeze damage, this being a limiting factor on highbush production in Maine.

Of those produced in Maine, all are marketed as pick your own. Production amounts from 6000 to 9000 pounds per acre per year. Disease and insect problems are similar to those for lowbush berries, with mummy berry and another fungi dominating. Limited support is provided to highbush growers by David Handley and the staff at Highmoor Farm, a University of Maine research facility.

Kevin and Arlene Ham in Acton, and Pam Harndon in Wilton, each with about eight acres of cultivated bushes, are the largest producers of highbush berries in Maine. There is no organized association of highbush growers in the state, but some are members of the Maine Vegetable and Small Fruit Growers Association.

PART VI: ALTERNATIVE MANAGEMENT

The following are examples of smaller growers who are finding alternative marketing methods to improve the income and reduce production costs of growing blueberries.

39

Spruce Mountain Blueberries

There are many, a great many, rock-strewn fields and small hillsides—some very steep—where true Maine wild blueberries grow. Some may be as small as my father's quarter acre cranberry bog, from which we picked our annual supply, and provided for other family members, and neighbors, when the crop was adequate. Then there are the in-betweens, those like myself whose relatively small acreage would not support the present day requirements of management equipment that have increased production tenfold or more on the barrens and larger fields. I asked David Yarborough about options for those individuals not willing to accept planned obsolescence. He suggested I visit with Molly Sholes in West Rockport.

After my many years of association with wild lowbush blueberries, I should have known that the very words connote rock-strewn, often steep – steep hillsides and panoramic views. At a roadside dooryard where I stopped to ask directions, to her father's answer, "At the end of the paved road, continue on the dirt road for half a mile or more until you go under a power line, it is the next house, on the right," a young girl added, "It's up, up, up", and she emphasized it by reaching, and pointing high with her forefinger, higher with each up, until she stood on tiptoes.

Molly and her husband had retired to this old farm, the small fields of which were hugged by old rugged maple trees that help hold the soil among frequent ledge outcroppings. To my announcement that I would like to talk blueberries with her, she

Fields at Spruce Mountain.

Molly Sholes produces a variety of blueberry products under her
Spruce Mountain brand.

bluntly replied, "You do not make a living raising blueberries. They pay the taxes." When I explained why I was there and that David Yarborough had suggested I see her, with an unnecessary apology that there were grandchildren in the house, I was invited in. Now widowed, but not willing to give-up on blueberries, Molly purchased the necessary equipment for cleaning, processing, and packaging an attractive line of canned blueberry recipes.

While we talked, the phone rang, and Molly took an order from a new customer in Old Orchard. Her wholesale business had steadily increased, and well it should. Her products are attractive packages of a product that is now getting most favorable mention for its food value. Molly and her neighbors are now being pressed on all sides by real estate developers who have a waiting market, not for the blueberries, but for the ocean vista.

Molly told me of a new generation of blueberry poachers, or more specific, rustlers: wild turkeys! Most of us have looked upon the revival of wild turkeys with pleasure and approval, but Molly assured me that they are clean and fast rakers, that a flock of a dozen or more, like soldiers marching in line, will pick a swath into a blueberry field, leaving few if any berries, until they are frightened away.

From the rapid spread of increasing numbers of wild turkeys, now often seen in flocks of forty or more, protected from hunting at the present time, there appears to be conflict in the future. No fence, as with deer, will keep them out. Will we have to reintroduce wolves to balance Nature?

Like so many agricultural pursuits, reminiscent of living off the land, there will be a final generation whose members will find a way to survive in order to enjoy the advantages of more freedom and less chaos in their daily lives, by maintaining a patch of wild blueberries on a steep hillside with an ocean vista, between rocks of all sizes and many shades of color.

40

THE STAPLES HOMESTEAD

Recently someone sent me an eight-page booklet of recipes for Wild Maine blueberries. It was interesting because of the title: Staples Homestead Wild Maine Blueberries. The surname was the same as mine, and of added interest, the owners were identified as Basil and Mary Staples. Basil is also my brother's first name.

Returning home from "Blueberryland," I came by way of Stockton Springs, the address given on the booklet. I inquired at the post office, and was directed to the County Road. Thinking it to be near to where County Road turned off from Route 1A, I drove on, passing several well-kept homes situated at the lower edge of a high ridge of blueberry fields. Wondering if I'd gone too far, I drove up the paved driveway to one of the homes where a gray-whiskered man stood in the open garage door. At my question, he provided directions to the Staples Homestead. We talked of blueberries. He invited me to walk to the top of his blueberry field, where the view would include the buildings belonging to the G.M. Allen and Sons blueberry processing plant in Orland, far across the Penobscot River, at the head of Penobscot Bay. The climb was too steep and too high for me, but I thanked him for his offer to share his far and beautiful view that I would have been proud to own.

The Staples Homestead was on the County Road, a mile or more past Blueberry Lane, over and around steep hills and resulting valleys. Many of the hillsides are open blueberry fields, most of which will not soon, if ever, be raked by mechanical equipment. The helicopter spraying of herbicides, fertilizers, and fungicides,

Blueberry field at the Staples Homestead. Photo by Spiros Polemis, courtesy Basil Staples..

nor anything else, has diminished the numbers and sizes of gray-white rocks that still add to the picturesque beauty of these hillside-hilltop blueberry fields.

Basil Staples was not at home, suggesting, and providing reason enough to return to this local "Blueberryland."

Eventually, I learned that Basil and Mary Staples lived in a relatively new home built on the bank of the Penobscot River; that their daughter and her family now live at the Staples Homestead. Basil, now retired, is a frequent workman on the blueberry land on the hilltop back of the Homestead. Yes, the Peter Staples who was granted land in Eliot (When it was Kittery, Mass. in the 1600s) appears to be a common genetic ancestor.

Like so many of the smaller blueberry growers, Basil had leased his land to a blueberry processor, and after consecutive harvests where he ended up owing money rather than seeing a profit, he considered alternative methods of management. The processor cooperated, limiting their contract to half of the field, while

Basil went organic with the remaining ten acres. In addition, he also established a pick your own marketing program. It was slow going at the start, but sales doubled, then re-doubled, as he advertised in the *Bangor Daily News* and got considerable coverage in magazines (including *Martha Stewart's Living)* and newspapers. His recipe booklet and a series of postcards have added to the profits, and he has also gradually added money-making conveniences for the pickers, such as boxes and carriers (and blueberry wine).

Basil and Mary Staples may well be the first organic blueberry grower marketing as pick your own, and their apparent success may well become a model for others to follow.

1992 Blueberry Production

Blueberry production in Maine set an all time record in 1992. New England Agricultural Statistics Service estimated the crop to be 85 million pounds, but other sources indicate the crop closer to 80 million pounds. Maine has exceeded Michigan in blueberry production in three out of the past five years. This year Maine produced 31 percent of the total blueberry crop in North America and exceeded Canadian production by more than 50 percent.

Wild Blueberry Newsletter, December 1992

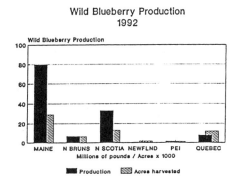

Wild Blueberry Production 1992

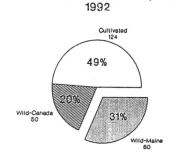

North American Blueberry Pie 1992

Wild Blueberry Baking and Handling Tips
Courtesy Basil Staples

• Wild blueberries have only 42 calories per 1/2 cup and contain vitamins A and B, as well as calcium, iron, and potassium.

• Wild blueberries are a favorite for baking because of their vibrant color and ability to maintain their shape.

• Fresh wild blueberries are perishable and should be refrigerated until ready to be used.

• When chilled and covered, fresh wild blueberries will last for two weeks at peak flavor.

• Do not wash blueberries before freezing. The secret to freezing wild blueberries is to freeze them when they are completely dry. Just pour into plastic containers.

• When freezing moist blueberries, place them in layers on a cookie sheet. As soon as they are frozen, they can be packed into plastic bags or containers.

• When used for baking, frozen berries don't have to be thawed before using.

• Frozen wild blueberries store well for two years without losing their flavor. They should not be refrozen if thawed.

Selected recipes

Wild Blueberry Muffins

Mix together	1 3/4 cups flour
	2/3 cup sugar
	1/2 tsp. salt
	3 tsp. baking powder
Add to the above	2 eggs
	1/2 cup milk
	1/4 cup vegetable oil
Add	1 cup wild blueberries

Bake at 350 for 25 minutes. Makes 12 muffins.

Wild Blueberry Cobbler

4 cups wild blueberries	1 egg, beaten
1/4 cup butter, cut in bits	1/4 tsp. salt
3/4 cup sugar	1/4 cup milk
3 tsp. lemon juice	1 tsp. vanilla
1 tsp. grated lemon	1 cup flour
5 tbs. butter	3 tsp. baking powder
1/4 cup sugar	1/4 tsp. nutmeg

Butter a two-quart baking dish. Combine blueberries, sugar, butter bits, lemon juice and rind. Pour into baking dish. Cream 5 tbs. butter with 1/4 cup sugar and salt. Add beaten egg. Mix with milk and vanilla. Stir in flour mixture with baking powder. Do not overmix. Spoon this dough mixture on top of the berries. Sprinkle with nutmeg and 1 tbs. sugar. Bake at 400 degrees got 25-30 minutes until biscuit topping is brown.

Blueberry-Apple Jelly

2 cups wild blueberries	3 tbs. lemon juice
1 box SureJell	2 cups apple juice
2 cups water	5 cups sugar

Crush berries and combine with water and lemon juice in saucepan. Bring to a slow boil and simmer 5 minutes. Squeeze out the juice using cheesecloth or jelly bag. Measure two cups into pan; if necessary add to water to make two cups. Add SureJell and apple juice, place over high heat, and stir until mixture comes to a hard boil. Immediately stir in sugar. Bring to a full rolling boil and boil for one minute, stirring often. Remove from heat. Skim off foam and pour into glasses and seal. Makes 8 six oz. glasses.

Basil Staples at work with his winnower.

41

STEVE CUMMINGS

Steve Cumming's blueberry field is high on King Hill in the town of South Paris, County of Oxford, Maine, about as far inland and westerly as blueberries are apt to do well in the state. There are about two hundred individually owned blueberry fields in the southwest corner of Maine, a few over the line in New Hampshire. Most, if not all, of them are serviced by Cherryfield Foods, from their field office in Gray, Maine. Until freezing became the major processing method for blueberries, Stewarts, at their canning plant in South Paris, purchased and canned the berries.

Cummings started selling berries—raked and winnowed carefully, with a Rivers winnower—to storekeepers, restaurants, and individuals, who came to the field during harvesting. Cherryfield Foods purchases any surplus berries he has.

Cummings is the publisher and distributor of *Blueberry News*, a letter-size single page containing blueberry recipes and notes of interest, which he gives and sends out to customers. He credits his sister with the idea and for producing it—on blue paper, of course. The fact that a copy was sent along and eventually got to me is evidence that it has advertising value for him.

He can depend upon family members and neighbors to rake his berries, and at times has taken his crew as far as Conway, New Hampshire, to rake for Cherryfield Foods. By doing his own mowing, raking, and some of the weed control, he keeps enough of the production costs as labor income, so that with the retail sales, he can afford to raise blueberries, but he readily admits that it is a way of life, rather than a way to make money.

Fortunately, the blueberries are but a small part of his 300-acre farm; most of the rest is well cared for woodland. The trees, and the blueberries were there when Steve's grandfather made a living on the farm 100 years ago, and the love and respect for the land remains in the family genes.

With his blueberry fields surrounded by woodland, I asked if he had any trouble from bear, deer, or wild turkeys scrounging for the ripe berries. He answered that those wild animals were often seen in the fields, and that on occasion, if too many of them came to snack, he would fire a shotgun blast or two over their heads to scare them away. He did not bother them at night, when undoubtedly they were sampling the berry crop, but unlike a relative—whose shot heard on an August evening may result in venison for his family—Steve accepts, actually welcomes, the wild animal forages as a part of the natural way of all life, and he enjoys the co-existence.

1992 Blueberry Production

Blueberry production in Maine set an all time record in 1992. New England Agricultural Statistics Service estimated the crop to be 85 million pounds, but other sources indicate the crop closer to 80 million pounds. Maine has exceeded Michigan in blueberry production in three out of the past five years. This year Maine produced 31 percent of the total blueberry crop in North America and exceeded Canadian production by more than 50 percent.

Wild Blueberry Newsletter, December 1992

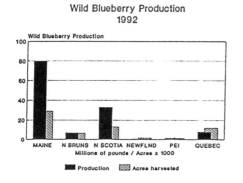

Wild Blueberry Production
1992

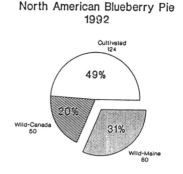

North American Blueberry Pie
1992

Blueberry News

Recipes from Mary Briggs, courtesy Steve Cummings

Wild Blueberry Bundt Cake

1 1/4 cups wild blueberries
3 cups flour
1 1/2 tsp. baking powder
1/4 tsp. baking soda
1/4 tsp. salt
3/4 cup softened margarine
1 cup sugar
4 eggs
1 cup non-fat yogurt
1 1/2 tsp. vanilla
2 Tbs. sugar as topping.

Stir dry ingredients. Cream margarine and sugar until fluffy. Add eggs, one at a time, beating well after each addition. Add vanilla. Add yogurt alternately with flour mixture, ending with flour. Mix well. Fold in blueberries. Pour into prepared bundt pan or 10" tube pan. Sprinkle remaining sugar over batter. Bake in prepare oven one hour. Cool cake in pan for 20 minutes.

Blueberry Crumb Pie

4 cups wild blueberries
3 Tbs. flour
pinch cinnamon or nutmeg

1/2 cup sugar
1 Tbs. lemon juice

topping
1/2 cup flour
1/2 cup butter or margarine
Single 9" pie crust

1/2 cup brown sugar

Mix blueberries, flour, sugar, and lemon juice and pour into prepared pie crust. (If using frozen berries, mix and then let sit about 15 minutes before pouring into crust.) Top berries with crumb mixture. Bake in preheated 400 degree oven for 40-50 minutes or until filling bubbles slightly. If topping and crust brown too quickly, cover lightly with foil for the last 15 minutes. Serve plain or with ice cream.

Finnish Blueberry Bars

Filling

2 1/2 cups wild blueberries	4 tbs. sugar
1 tbs. lemon juice	2 tbs. cornstarch
pinch salt	

Crust

2 1/2 cups flour	1/2 sup sugar
1 egg, lightly beaten	1/2 tsp. baking powder
1 cup soft butter, not margarine	

1tbs. sugar as topping.

Mix blueberries, sugar, lemon juice, cornstarch, and salt. Set aside. Blend flour, sugar, egg, and baking powder in a large bowl. Cut in butter until mixture resembles fine crumbs. With hands, press together to make dough. Roll half on lightly floured 10 x 14 cookie sheet. Form a ridge around rim to filling will not run out. Spread filling over dough in pan. Roll out remainder of dough to one-eighth inch thickness. Cut into strips and place in lattice-work fashion over filling. Dough can bed crumbly but can be pieced together. Sprinkle lightly with sugar. Bake at 375 degrees for 25-30 minutes. Cut into squares.

42

CHRIS McCORMICK

When the land values and the taxes increased, and neighboring fields became viewing lots, Chris McCormick sold his property in West Rockport and moved his family to an old farm in the town of Cooper, a more remote area in eastern Washington County. An experienced cabinet maker, with timber cut from the property, he transformed a barn on the property into an attractive home, and he now has a shop under construction that will temporarily house the equipment necessary to process, freeze, and package Maine organic, wild lowbush blueberries for the retail market.

The framed, walled, and roofed structure is actually that of a house that will become the family home when the blueberry business is able to support construction of a building suitable for processing.

In the meantime, a careful observer might recognize the built-in Rivers winnower as an integral part of the blueberry cleaning equipment now dominating the interior building space. Powered by an electric motor, he has it synchronized so that it winnows, and controls the flow of berries onto the inspection table and then on to the packaging area.

Chris rakes his blueberries using a hand-powered machine that resembles a hand-pushed lawn mower, with the rake teeth protruding from the front. By pulling a lever near the handles, the berries are dumped into a standard removable blueberry half-bushel box nested just back of the bicycle wheels on which the machine is supported. The level of the rake teeth is controlled from the handle bars, the wheel axle acting as a fulcrum.

Chris McCormick with his modified raker. Photo by Natalie Peterson.

Steve McCormick's winnower and cleaning equipment. Photo by Natalie Peterson.

Chris McCormick is another owner of a small lowbush blueberry acreage who believes he has found a way to continue the way of self-reliance in a country setting for himself and his family. He is an individual with ideas and ambition second only to his love of the land and the daily commune with nature.

BLUEBERRIES

The maple leaves
    And pumpkins gone,
The fields are red
    Where berries grew
Between the rocks
    On highest hills;
Some blue with fruit
    At harvest time,
And backs were sore
    From raking them.
It seems they save
    Their beauty days
Until the frost
    Has browned all else.
Their leaves stay on
    When others gone
And turning red
    Then paint the fields,
Identify
    Where bees will work
And berries set
Come Spring again.

43

SUMMARY

Blueberry fields in Maine increased to about 60,000 acres when the fish canning factories along the coast changed to canning blueberries during the harvest, but gradually decreased to 50,000 acres, then again increased to 64,000 acres due to improved growing management, insect and disease control measures, processing improvements (freezing) and marketing efforts.

The figures are impressive: 7.1 cents per pound paid for 4.136 million pounds grown in 1924, to 47.4 cents (five year average) paid for 110.6 million pounds in the year 2000. Much of this increase was due to the cooperating efforts of industry and the University of Maine Cooperative Extension and supporting services. This especially includes the marketing group, Wild Blueberry Association of North America (WBANA).

It is not my desire or intent to belittle the commercial successes evident from the foregoing figures, but I confess to a tinge of nostalgia for what has been lost as a part of the price paid for greater production and distribution of Maine wild lowbush blueberries. It is similar to the changes in other agricultural production throughout the nation, be it dairy, potatoes, orchards. It is inevitable.

Bill Guptill suggested that the young people left the farms in Wesley because their parents wanted them to get a better education, and could afford to send the children off to college. Most of them got positions away from home, due to their education and did not come back to Wesley. It was, of course, a lot more than that.

Mechanical burning.

Cars, trucks, mechanized equipment, state and federal regulations, and much more, including the number of children in the families, all played a part.

With three or more tractor-driven mechanical rakers, a blueberry field is harvested today in less than half the time than it might take with fifty hand rakers, many of them children, spotting the field . The smell and sound of diesel motors and clanking of metal equipment have replaced the fresh air, voices, and laughter. The family labor income on small farms has been replaced with hired mechanized equipment, by chemicals to control diseases that require trained and licensed applicators. No more Micmac Indians are joined by the landowner family to sing and dance by campfire light outside their tents at the edge of a blueberry field of a warm August night. In short, for many, a way of life has changed dramatically.

There are probably more than 500 such small farms with blueberry fields in Maine. Many of them will not go away. Some will survive by lease or management agreements with one of the larger processors. But some will find a way to stay on the farm, managing their blueberry fields in some way to pay the taxes.

My lease provides that I and my family may mark off an area

Mechanical raking.

for personal use and rake an adequate supply of free berries, where I can practice the art of raking blueberries, watch out for the return of Princess, occasionally see a bear or deer or fox, be out where the smell and sight of berries enhance the pleasures of an August morning.

Wesley is still Blueberryland. It is but one of many towns whose rolling hill fields are blue in August, the fall leaf color reflecting red in October, and harvested patches burned black in late fall and spring. The fields are spotted over an area twenty miles inland, the length of the Maine seacoast, from Eastport to Kittery. Blueberries are commercially produced primarily Downeast in Washington and Hancock counties, and most on the barrens.

I had thought that mechanized raking spelled the planned obsolescence of the small blueberry grower, but I was wrong. Some, maybe many of them, will survive because of their love of the land, and their ability to find a way to maintain that very special Way of Life.

MAINE BLUEBERRY PRODUCTION (MILLIONS) AND PRICE

Year	Lbs.	Cents	Year	Lbs.	Cents	Year	Lbs.	Cents
1924	4.136	7.1	1953	12.168	13.0	1981	21.746	42.3
1925	6.605	8.0	1954	22.560	12.2	1982	35.925	52.0
1926	7.104	8.6	1955	15.971	9.1	1983	44.700	37.0
1927	10.066	7.5	1956	16.496	12.3	1984	24.680	25.0
1928	6.096	7.8	1957	29.354	12.3	1985	43.700	23.0
1929	7.344	8.3	1958	16.298	14.6	1986	42.000	31.0
1930	15.496	5.3	1959	22.607	12.2	1987	36.33	45.0
1931	9.878	2.6	1960	21.336	12.3	1988	52.3	50
1932	4.889	2.5	1961	25.550	11.1	1989	26.8	50
1933	8.173	4.7	1962	30.282	10.2	1990	75.3	37
1934	5.622	4.1	1963	22.795	12.1	1991	39.5	46
1935	6.070	3.7	1964	21.863	13.2	1992	84.6	41
1936	7.416	5.8	1965	10.607	19.9	1993	64.6	28
1937	13.955	6.4	1966	19.342	17.0	1994	59.5	30
1938	7.929	3.1	1967	28.857	10.1	1995	65.9	32
1939	6.872	3.5	1968	13.645	13.5	1996	59.2	57
1940	12.559	5.4	1969	19.571	14.9	1997	73.8	43
1941	16.990	7.3	1970	9.167	20.0	1998	62.9	46
1942	11.933	8.0	1971	19.154	16.3	1999	65.9	51
1943	17.395	12.9	1972	16.928	22.2	2000	110.6	40
1944	3.503	16.2	1973	22.096	26.9			
1945	8.815	18.6	1974	18.566	18.5			
1946	11.238	19.3	1975	11.910	26.5			
1947	12.475	11.1	1976	24.908	31.0			
1948	17.750	11.2	1977	14.369	60.6			
1949	15.158	11.6	1978	18.053	51.0			
1950	14.668	12.4	1979	17.575	36.0			
1951	26.860	12.3	1980	21.190	38.0			
1952	8.071	12.0						

Source: 1924-1989 Maine Department of Agriculture (1924-1928 includes imported berries. 1990-2000 New England Agricultural Statistics service.

BLUEBERRY HARVEST

It's berry time again.
The rocky pasture slopes
Where children clanged their rakes
And cleared the tines of hay
While chatter filled the air
Now thick with alder sprouts.
But fields where hay once cut.
Hay stored to Winter feed
The horses and the ox,
Those fields a solid blue
And clean of weeds and grass.
The muffled motors chug
As drums of teeth respond
    While harvesting the crop.

44

ADOPTED TOWN

One could not have observed a town and its people over a period of more than sixty years, without having accumulated considerable knowledge of the geographic and habitat changes as they took place. Wesley was a well known and popular deer hunting area, with Harold Day's Airline Inn for sportsmen, with which I became acquainted on my first visit to Wesley in 1937. My memories include getting there, the hunting trips, and the few families who lived on Day Hill who were involved with deer hunting.

The 75-mile-long, unimproved road—hardly more than dirt wheel tracks with grass and an occasional bush growing up between—that wove around swamps and lakes and over steep hillsides; the trees each side with limbs that brushed passing vehicles; and bridges, with loose and missing planks, over substantial streams, required four hours driving time. Speed was slow enough that deer were in no danger of being hit by a vehicle, and they were often seen standing in the road, watching our approach.

Though natives of Maine, members of our hunting parties, including myself, were awed by the seemingly endless forest of fir and spruce, old growth beech trees on the ridges, the number of deer, the occasional bear, many partridge, and the plentiful spawning trout in the streams we crossed. Though Township 26 being only a small part of the forest area of the state, we became, after spending annual November weeks walking over the ridges, heaths, and burned areas, very familiar with those surroundings.

Granddaughter Alison and friend picking blueberries.

Fully as impressive were the open fields of wild lowbush blue-berries that extended both sides of the road down the hillsides to the distant forest. No less were the friendships that developed with the residents of Day Hill whom we met: Thatcher Guptill, his wife, and his family of four sons and two daughters; Harold Day at the Airline Inn, his wife and son Buddy that first year, and in later years, Carl and Eleanor Day, Phil Durling, Otis Carlow, Paul Seavey; the Guptills of Guptill Road; and Thurle and Dolly Hanson (who ran the little store in Crawford).

The amount of my time spent in Wesley increased consider-ably after my sons, and a few friends gathered and built a cabin in nearby Crawford. We named it HOWDEE. It was our camp, built of native pine according to our sketched design, every plank placed, every nail pounded in and the roof covered by ourselves. I built the sink area and added the pitcher pump to bring water from the dug well. I built the table, the benches, and the bed-steads. Son Mark installed the electric wiring, and we heated the camp and cooked our meals on an ancient black iron wood-burning kitchen stove. The deer and rabbit hunting in winter, and the bass and perch fishing in summer lured us to return at every opportunity.

But it was my experience managing my fifteen acre blueberry field and the response of the local families to my needs during the blueberry harvest periods of August that led to my becoming *adopted*.

Though Route 9 has become a major Canadian access highway from Bangor to the Atlantic Provinces, and Thatcher Guptill has died and his house burned, following generations have taken their places. Thatcher's daughter, Nellie, who was thirteen years-old that first year we had breakfast in their house, later married local Bill Haywood, and inherited some of her father's blueberry fields, and like myself, is now a grandparent. The original Guptill Farm on Guptill Road is still Guptill's generations later, and a major blueberry processing and freezer storage plant has been built by the road on that first blueberry field I walked across on my way to the hunting cabin five miles back in the spruce and fir forest, on 'Possum Pond.

Much more than having read the history of the town, it has been hearing the stories told by Eleanor Day, the white perch fishing with Phil Durling, hunting with Thatcher's sons, taking eels with Paul Seavey from his traps at Pokey Dam, and the hours of blueberry talk that has given me a feeling of being a part of the town, one I have much appreciated and enjoyed.